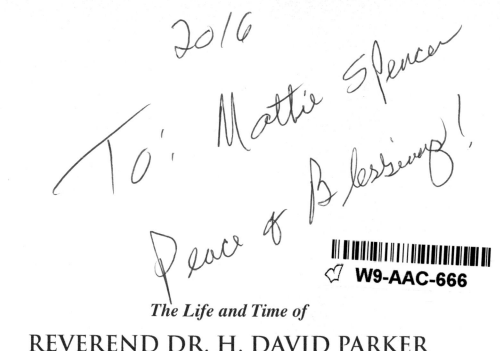

2016

To: Mattie Spencer

Peace & Blessings!

H. David Parker

Lady "P"

The Life and Time of

REVEREND DR. H. DAVID PARKER

GOD'S VISIONARY AMBASSADOR

REVEREND HERBERT DAVID PARKER

EXULON ELITE

INTRODUCTION

T he contents of the book, "The Life and Times of Rev. Dr. H. David Parker: God's Visionary Ambassador," are reflections of the life and legacy of an anointed and prophetic Gospel preacher. Each chapter and page of his writing will captivate the mind and hearts of readers, as well as convey his life story.

From the first time that I met Pastor Parker, he was speaking of his life's journey. He would tell stories of his time on the farm; his life in the military; his calling to preach, and his life as a moderator. The stories were told continuously; days, months, and then years. As his wife of twenty-five years, my response was always, "Put it in a book" so that we could read it to our children in later years. Finally, in January 2001, at the age of eighty, he began to record his life's journey. Even though Dr. Parker went home to be with the Lord, this book will serve as a divinely inspired legacy for anyone whom God has called to lead a life of impact.

I believe the hand of God, through divine providence, was leading Dr. Parker, a farm boy, from the cotton fields of Alabama to becoming the Representative to the United Nation for the National Baptist Convention. It is my belief that God knew at birth that this man of wisdom and dignity would influence and enlighten the lives of generations.

The benevolent mercy of God does not happen in one's life by accident. It is stated in His Holy Word, "Before I formed thee in the belly I knew thee; and before thou camest forth out of the womb I sanctified thee, and I ordained thee a prophet unto the nations." (Jeremiah 1:5).

"God's Visionary Ambassador" discloses the dedication and commitment of a faithful and true servant of God. The central purpose is to leave a memoir for others to substantiate that God never fails; to encourage preachers to preach the unadulterated Gospel of Jesus Christ, and lastly, to motivate all to walk in the ways of the Lord. It is informative, inspirational and transformative to those who have dedicated their lives in pursuit of God's purpose. "God's Visionary Ambassador" is authentic and represents a real-life example of vision, commitment and leadership.

It is my sincere prayer that those who are reading this book will gain a vast appreciation from the writings of a sage leader of courage and insight. As a testament to the word of Theodore Epps, "Our strength is seen in the things we stand for; our weakness is seen in the things we fall for." Dr. Parker's life's journey attests to the fact that one does not have to compromise to succeed, but to be faithful and dedicated to the cause for Christ.

Lady Flora Covington-Parker

ACKNOWLEDGEMENTS

I give thanks and praise to the Almighty God, for His grace and unconditional love. I could not have mastered this life's pilgrimage without Him. I thank the many people who encouraged me to write this book; my life story. I pray that it will be a source of inspiration, which you will be able to share with generations to come. I encourage you to keep it in the archives of your home, so that everyone will have easy access.

Special thanks to my family and friends for their prayers. Life is a journey, which takes years to sort out and make the experiences come alive. I have spent many years writing: I started with handwriting, typewriting, and later advanced to Windows. Nevertheless, the information given is from a heart of prayer, love and meditation.

I am ninety-three years of age now, and the mind does not operate as it did in earlier years. I am confident that this book will be completed and published at the appropriate time; God's time. I have been on the battlefield a long time, and have always received the favor of God.

Reverend Dr. H. David Parker, one of God's anointed, went home to be with the Lord the first of the year 2015, approximately two months prior to his ninety-fourth birthday. Yes, he had all intentions of completing his memoir. He always knew that he could count on me, his wife Flora, to get it in the hands of a publisher. I would love to see the expression on his face, were he alive, to witness the  publication of this book. I am sure it would be a "Kodak" moment. I must say that during my time of despondency, it gave me strength to have a project to look forward to; something that I knew was of the utmost importance. I want to thank those who have contributed to this endeavor: I thank the pastors and co-laborers in Christ for their expressions and words of encouragement. Thanks to Bishop Phillip Elliott, pastor of the Antioch Baptist Church Cathedral of Hempstead; Darren Greggs, Program Director, New York's #1 Gospel Radio Station, WTHE 1520; my niece, E. Faye Wright, for her expressions; and my sister, Bernice Covington, for her assistance. Special thanks to my skillful proofreader and sorority sister, Maxine Reynolds Jennings, a Virginia State University alumna and retired Baltimore City educator, for her proficiency, deleting, crossing T's and dotting I's. All of you were a tower of strength. Yes, it has been a year of experiences compiling information, searching through computer files, boxes, file cabinets, and yes, calling his sisters: Ethel, Alma, and Ruth for clarification. I have no complaints, only a heart of thanksgiving. I believe this was the divine will of God, for such a time as this. It was He who gave me the strength and wisdom to complete this task. *"You've got to get up every morning with determination, if you're going to go to bed with satisfaction."* (**George Horace Lorimer**)

FOREWORD

"Na o day is well spent without a talk with God." These familiar words rang out as Reverend Dr. H. David Parker warmed the hearts of his radio audience day after day, month after month, and year after year. His years of experience and wealth of spiritual wisdom placed him in a rank of high esteem as he pastored the Emmanuel Baptist Church of Elmont, New York for some forty-five years. His life was filled with intriguing feats that he was always proud to reflect on. This, his personal memoir, carries the reader through his rich personal history with his signature gift of storytelling. The stories that he told always had a jewel of wisdom to accompany them. Reverend Parker was a great man of God who could teach any preacher something new with each sermon. This narrative promises to illustrate his strong character, his abiding faith in God, and his unyielding commitment to spread the Good News of Jesus Christ.

Reverend Parker's knowledge of the Word of God had a way of inching into the crevices of any preacher's brain that had never been touched. No matter if they were experienced on the topic or not, they gained a new nugget of knowledge after every conversation or sermon. I believe that being under the voice of many of Reverend Parker's sermons, lectures, and speeches has made me the much enabled preacher and teacher that I am today. Being under Reverend Parker's tutelage has taught me new ways to successfully pour into others. I am still mastering these skills today as I carry out my ministry. I pride myself on being able to pour into others as Reverend Dr. H. David Parker was so willing to pour into me.

Bishop Phillip E. Elliott, Pastor

Antioch Baptist Cathedral

Hempstead, New York

CONTENTS

Chapter One

THE EARLY YEARS

I t was in the year 1921, February 27th to be exact, that I made my entrance into this world by divine appointment. The second of eight children, born to George Lemon Parker and Laura Bell Brown-Parker, in a little wooden shack at a location known as "The Old Taylor Place," near the little hamlet of Jones, Alabama. A very humble beginning and one upon which I have often reflected since my early childhood.

Because of the many suggestions and encouraging words that I have received from many of my close relatives, friends and associates, I have sought to set in all, as best I can, a history of my life; biography or autobiography as the information dictates.

I must thank, first of all, my first wife, Willie Mae Bates-Parker, with whom I shared a life of thirty-four-and-a-half years and who bore for me six lovely children. It was she who urged me early on to put on paper my life experiences for future generations to ponder. But it was not until her passing and God brought into my life another charming, intelligent and supporting person to be my helpmeet, in the person of Flora D. Covington-Parker. From the first years of our marriage, she has constantly encouraged me to begin writing my life's story.

So here I begin: it is Tuesday evening, January 23, 2001, at 6:45 in the evening, on the thirteenth floor of the Renaissance Hotel in Nashville, Tennessee. Flora and I are attending the Mid-Winter Board Meeting of the National Baptist Convention, USA, Inc. This is the beginning of my life's story and it is my prayer that the Holy Spirit will guide me as I reflect on the past; my early childhood memories and up until this present time, only one month from my eightieth birthday.

Well, what are my early memories? As I mentioned earlier, my birthplace was in the community known as "The Old Taylor Place." I was about two years of age, probably in 1923, when my mother was in the field working about a quarter of a mile from the shack where she had left me and my two brothers. As I recall, there was a donkey, mule or horse left outside of the house, and when the animal began to bray, I was frightened out of my wits. I ran off of the porch and proceeded down the small hill toward my parents. This experience will stay with me for a long time.

We moved from the Old Taylor Place to the farm of Mr. Caesar Bishop, approximately six or seven miles from the Old Taylor Place. My parents moved there in an attempt to better their conditions. At that time, they were the parents of three sons: John Samuel, Herbert "D," and Walter Love. We spent one year on Mr. Bishop's place, working on half; i.e., we were supposed to receive half of what was made on the farm. But this never occurred. And two or three things stand out in my mind about our experience there. First, my father shooting a dog to death with his twelve-gauge shot gun. The dog had been stealing our eggs for a number of weeks. One afternoon, after he had robbed the hen nest, my father rushed into the house and retrieved his shotgun. As the dog was running with an egg in his mouth, my father cut him down with one shot. Secondly, on Mr. Bishop's farm, I was picking cotton; although I was just a three-year-old lad, I was good at "cotton picking." The last thing I remember on Mr. Bishop's farm was my father falling from a mule and getting caught in the harness and almost dragged to death. Had it not been for one of his friends, Mr. Phillip Johnson, who was standing in the path where the mule was galloping with my father in the tow, and stopped the mule, my father would have been dragged to his death. These are the three incidents that I vividly recall while at the Bishop farm.

My father and mother spent only one year on Mr. Bishop's farm; we then moved to another location called "The Taylor Place." The first memory was of the "Old Taylor Place." Now we were at the new location. We arrived at this location in 1924, and one year later, my sister, Ethel Mae, was born. Now there were three sons and one daughter, and we lived in a two-room shack; wooden floors with one-inch cracks. We were required to walk a quarter of a mile for drinking water. I was only four years of age and my older brother was five years of age, we began to understand the word "poverty" or "poor." As I said earlier, my parents were blessed with eight children; four sons and four daughters. All eight of us were born with the aid of a midwife. None had the privilege of being born in a hospital and attended by a physician. Where to from here?

The family remained at the "Taylor Place" until the fall of 1929. While here, two other siblings were born, Tommie Lee and Alma Lillian. It was here that two of us began our education. Except for the first day when our father drove us to the Julius Rosenwald School at the New Salem Baptist Church, we were required to walk the three miles each day. How well do I remember that first day? When our father dropped us off at school using his buggy and horse, when he departed, I rushed to the window to wave him "good-bye." It was at that point that the principal tapped me on the head with a ruler and ordered me to sit down, informing me that I was in school. There were only two classrooms, one principal and one teacher. How can one forget these memories? While attending school and continuing to farm there at the "Taylor Place," we had some wonderful neighbors: Mr. Albert Lanier and his family; Mr. Walter Love and his family; and, of course, my grandparents.

My first remembrance of church was New Salem Baptist Church. It was at New Salem where I first learned how to behave in church. It was not uncommon for parents during those days to literally discipline an unruly child in the church by resorting to a switch or belt, even while the preacher was delivering his sermon. How many times did I observe a mother taking an unruly child outside of the church and tanning his or her backside to bring him or her under control? There was neither pouting nor disrespect toward, not only the mother or father, but any adult. Calling the police was unheard off. Personally, I am not sure if it would have made a difference.

Now we moved from the Taylor Place near Jones, Alabama, to Enoch Weldon's farm near Billingsley, Alabama. How well do I recall that my two brothers and I drove the livestock; cows and hogs the eight or ten miles from the Taylor Place to the Weldon Place. When we arrived there in late November or December 1929, we took up residence in a small wooden bungalow house with only three small rooms. Mom and Dad occupied the main room, or the front room; the four boys occupied one room, and our little sister, Ethel, shared the room with Mom and Dad. It was here that we were exposed, for the first time, to cars passing the house once or twice during the day. It was always an exciting time to observe a Model T Ford coming down the road. We children would run to the road and wave at the car as it passed. It was here also that my father worked on halves with Mr. Weldon. It was here that I learned that regardless of how hard we worked, we never seemed to achieve anything. We did not have much; God took care and watched over the family. My father would shop at Mr. Weldon's store during the year, and at the end of the year, Mr. Weldon would tally the books.

My father always "broke about even." Regardless of how many bales of cotton, how much corn, how much other farm products were harvested, it was always just enough to break even. How many times did my mother cook, wash, and iron all day for Mrs. Weldon to be paid with a gallon of milk and a pound of butter at the end of the day. Not only was this our experience, but it was the same experience other tenants confronted on the "Weldon Farm."

Well, it was while we were tenants on Mr. Weldon's plantation that I was converted; "got religion," was saved! It was in the summer of 1932, on a Monday evening while attending the Fall Revival at the New Mount Zion Baptist Church in Billingsley, Alabama. I never shall forget the experience. My dear mother and her friend, Mrs. Ann Mall, were leading in the devotional service when I had a conversion experience. With my brothers and others at the mourners' bench, I was conversing with a young lady that I took to be my girlfriend, when all of a sudden I found myself standing and crying uncontrollable. No longer was I ashamed to cry out; no longer was I concerned about who was present. From that Monday night until Friday night, I could neither eat nor drink. My family, and especially my brothers, surmised that I had "lost it." It was not until that Friday night that I stood and gave my hand to the preacher, the Rev. B.J. Taylor, and confessed a hope in Jesus Christ, that I found peace. As the saying went then, I had "got religion."

On that Sunday, I was baptized in a small stream near the church; the only one baptized that year. When the service was over that Sunday afternoon, and I returned home to Mr. Weldon's farm, while sitting in the yard with my mother, I asked, "Mama, do that tree look different to you?" "Mama, look at my hands, do they look new to you?" So, at the age of eleven or twelve, the Lord had found me. We remained on Mr. Weldon's farm for about four or five years, and then moved to the farm of Mr. Charlie Forshee, near Clanton, Alabama. My sister, Ruth Estelle, was born. From this point, life began to take on new meaning.

It was on Mr. Forshee's farm that my father began to yearn for a better life for his family. The children were attending a one-room schoolhouse about six miles from the farm. We walked to school for the four or five months that we were permitted to attend school. We remained on Mr. Forshee's farm until the fall of 1938. It was at that time, the big push began to take place. My father uprooted the family, and moved to a small farm in the Chilton County community. Here is where my life began to change. Permit me to share some personal experiences here. I shall return, perhaps, to some early experiences.

After moving from the Forshee Farm near Billingsley, Alabama, my father had purchased a new horse for me to plough. It was in the spring of 1939, the month of March, to be sure. We had attended Sunday school that Sunday; the entire family. After returning from Sunday school, we, my brothers and I, John and Walter, decided to visit with the "Bryant Sisters." Now listen to this: there were three sisters: ages eighteen, seventeen, and sixteen. There were three Parker brothers: ages eighteen, seventeen, and sixteen.

On that Sunday afternoon, at about two o'clock, my older brother, John Samuel, made the suggestion that we would visit the Bryant Sisters. There would be a sister for each of us. As we proceeded from the house, my father asked, "Where 'yall goin?" We said, "To Mr. Bryant." His immediate response, and I can hear him now: "No you ain't!" Then he proceeded with a protracted argument, "You ain't going to start loafing." He went on and on for seemingly an hour. We continued to walk; my father continued to argue. Finally I said to my brothers, "Let's go back." My oldest brother, who we called "Dutch," said to me, "Are you scared?" I said, "No, but let's go back." I was seventeen years of age and he was eighteen. We turned back and it was at that juncture that I knew that it was time for me to leave home.

My father and I had experienced a previous confrontation. I was never disrespectful to him, but I remember that one Sunday morning he decided to drive the buggy to church; our former church. He asked me to hitch the horse to the buggy and to use the small collar on the horse. I followed his instructions to the tee. When he saw the horse and buggy ready to go, he said to me, "I told you to put the large collar on the horse." I then replaced the small collar with the large collar. He came out and prepared to enter the buggy. He then said to me, "I told you to put the small collar on the horse." At that point I said, "I wish you would make up your mind." In the twinkling of an eye, my father lashed out at me with a whip and left a scar on my ankle that I will take to my grave.

Many years later, after I became a man and had traveled almost the entire world, my father and I used to speak of those early days. I would mention to him some of the things that he did to us that I felt were unfair He would always apologize and say, "I did not know any better; I was doing the best that I could." I never held any animosity toward him. For a man with only a third grade education and striving to rear eight children on a farm, where he was forever cheated out of his labor, yes, he did the best that he could.

I need to reflect here that my early childhood was anything but pleasant. All we knew to do was work, work, and work! The opportunity for schooling was extremely limited. How well do I recall that when the time came for planting and harvesting the crops, we were taken out of school. While we were permitted to go to school, the "colored" children, as we were referred to then, had to walk four or five miles to school, while the "white" children were riding buses only two to three miles. Many times they would pass us on the road, open the windows and say to us, "Get out of the road, N— — —." By the grace of God, we made it.

In March 1939, as we began to prepare for the early spring plowing, I had decided that I no longer desired the life on the farm. I felt that it was time for me to flutter my wings, leave the comfortable environs of my parents (if it could be called that), and venture out into an unknown and hostile world. How was this to be accomplished? Well, a few days earlier, a notice had appeared in the local newspaper inviting young men from deprived families to join the C.C.C. (Civilian Conservation Corps). The sign-up period was the last week in March. How was I to make the cut-off date? I fabricated a story to my father, my mother being privy to the scheme, that I had a severe toothache and that I had to go to the dentist to have it extracted. Well, that morning, my mother and I went to the sign-up site. I took the test, and three or four days later, received a notice that I had passed and that I was to report to the site on April 4, 1939 for transportation to the camp site near Selma, Alabama. The site was known as "Alabama SP-10."

When the letter arrived at the house announcing the reporting date, it was laid on the mantle board above the fireplace in the living room of our shanty frame house. When my father came home for the evening, he retrieved the letter and read its contents. The first words that he said to my mother, "What is this?" He read it again and then began his usual tirade when things did not go his way. I was in the small back room, about seven o'clock in the evening, and I could hear him arguing. He said, "I just bought another mule for that boy to plow and he is talking about going to some C.C.C. camp. I won't sign it!"

The next day, my father consulted with one of his close friends by the name of Phillip Johnson. He informed Mr. Johnson that I had signed up for the C.C.C. camp and that he had just bought a new mule for me to help on the farm. Then he said to Mr. Johnson,

"I will not sign it," but I later learned that Mr. Johnson said to my father, "Son, why don't you sign the letter? He is now eighteen years old and he will run away from home anyway. You ought to sign it." That evening when my father came home, he signed the letter without saying a word to me and placed it back on the mantle board. I believe that was Friday, March 1, 1939. I was to leave on Monday, March 4, 1939.

Saturday and Sunday were filled with excitement for all of us. I went to church that Sunday, and when I returned home that afternoon I was filled with excitement, apprehension and uncertainty. That evening; Sunday evening, my mother packed a small bag of clothes for me and early that Monday morning she made me a sandwich. I walked out of the house that morning and started up a small hill on a dirt road from the house. When I arrived at the top of the hill, I looked back and saw my mother waving to me. I waved and began my journey through life as a man. I had not walked more than fifty yards when a flatbed truck stopped and gave me a ride into town. I was now on my own; no father to scream at me and no mother to encourage me. The Lord was guiding and protecting me as I journeyed along my way.

We arrived at Alabama State Park Number Ten some time that afternoon. We were given clean linen, clothing, and shown our sleeping quarters. There were four of us young men that left Clanton, Alabama; I was the youngest of the four. After we had been shown our quarters, we were told to prepare for supper; a

25

new experience for me. I had never experienced living with electric lights, running water, and indoor toilet facilities. It was amazing, to be sure. I spent the first afternoon and evening just admiring the sights and the place.

The next morning, we were up and ready to go at 6:00 a.m. Breakfast was served and we returned to our quarters to make our beds. We were given instructions as to how they should be made. Every item had to be aligned with the next bunk. Towels had to be folded a certain way; shoes were placed under bunks uniformly. Clothes were hung the same way; items of clothes that had buttons were required to be buttoned. It was discipline, it was training, and it was a daily regimen. It did not take long to adapt to and enjoy the discipline. One thing for sure, I did not have to plow all day in the field. I knew that the Lord would make a way, somehow.

I shall never forget this experience, and today I thank God for having led me this way. Lest I forget, the area policing that took place each morning after breakfast was more like a ceremony. We were admonished by our leader that if we saw something on the ground, if it did not grow, we were to pick it up: Cigarette butts, match stems, paper, leaves or anything that did not grow were to be picked up and placed in a container. The area surrounding our barracks (sleeping quarters) was immaculate at all times.

Following this ceremony, we were placed on trucks and taken to our place of work. The workday was from 9:00 a.m. until 3:00 p.m. I had never heard of such a thing; I was accustomed to working from sun-up until sundown. From 3:00 p.m. until time for dinner at 5:00 p.m., was time spent playing some type of games, checkers, basketball, pool, and learning to box (prize fight). Boxing was my first choice. The trainer laced up my gloves and those of my opponent, and placed us in the ring. When I moved forward to throw the first punch, my opponent just held out his glove. I ran into the glove and the next thing I remember, I was looking into the sky. That was the first and last time I ever had boxing gloves on my hands; a quick and easy lesson that has lasted a lifetime.

While at this camp site, Alabama SP-10, I was determined to make something of myself. It was the easiest lifestyle that I had ever experienced. It was at this site that I learned brick masonry. I learned to cut rocks, shape them to fit a certain location, and cement and lay them in place. We constructed a two-foot rock wall around a one-and-a-half-mile pond; perhaps the wall is still there. After serving at this location for a number of months, we were relocated to Citronelle, Alabama, Alabama State Park #SP-11. It was at this location that my life really began to take shape. Shortly after arriving there, I was placed in charge of the Medical Dispensary, where I dispensed aspirin and other items under the supervision of a contract physician.

The camp offered training for those who were interested, including typing. I was fascinated with the typewriter, for I had never used one before. After paying $1.50 for a three-month course, at the end of three months, I could type accurately seventy-five to eighty words per minute. The electric typewriter was not yet in use. This was a standard Royal typewriter, with the keys covered. We learned to touch type; i.e., could not see the letter on the keys. Having this knowledge has stood me in good stead through my life. I was soon promoted to assistant leader, and received a monthly increase in salary from $30 to $36. From the $30 per month salary, $22 was sent home to my parents and I survived on the remaining $8. When I received the salary increase to $36 per month, $24 was sent home to my parents and I survived on the remaining $12.

As my two-year stint was coming to a close, the camp commander stated that there was only one position for an individual to be promoted from assistant leader to leader, and that individual would be given a two-year extension. The kitchen steward and I, the first aid steward, competed for the promotion and the two-year extension. The camp commander flipped the coin and the kitchen steward won. So at the end of March 1941, I was discharged to return home. It was a sad day for me, but it was by divine appointment that I did not win. The Lord was guiding my footsteps.

Well, what would the future hold for me? I returned to my parents' home, but not to the farm. Incidentally, the money that had been sent to my parents while I was away in the C.C.C. assisted them in building a house, which stands until this day. After a few days there in Clanton, Alabama, I decided to relocate to Sylacauga, Alabama, and reside with my aunt, Mary Alice Goodgame. From mid-April 1941 until July or August 1941, I worked as a handyman in a grocery store and meat market. In late August or early September 1941, I began working at E.I. DuPont Defense Plant in Childersburg, Alabama. It was from there that I was drafted into the United States Army. You will read again in later writing that on September 4, 1942, I was sworn into the United States Army in Fort Benning, Georgia, where I began a military career that spanned more than twenty years. I retired with military honors, as a master sergeant from the United States Air Force on October 31, 1962.

I must back up here. On December 7, 1941, that bright and beautiful Sunday morning, I was playing a game of checkers at my aunt's home, when the news came over the radio that Japan had bombed Pearl Harbor. Of course, Pearl Harbor meant nothing to me. Throughout the day, the airways were filled with the sad news. President Roosevelt came over the radio and declared that the United States had declared war. Little did I know, at the time, that I was being prepared, not only for service to my country, but for service to God.

My Aunt, Mary Alice, my mother's youngest sister, permitted me to live with her without paying rent. At that time, I was earning $25.41 per week; excellent pay at the time. My aunt occupied the family home site; a four-bedroom beautiful colonial-type home. It had been left by my grandmother, Molly Brown, who owned an estate on the outskirts of Sylacauga, consisting of four houses beside the family home. In addition, she owned eighty acres of land two miles from the city line. My mother came from a fairly well-to-do family. My parents were married in 1919 in Talladega, Alabama, and my father and mother relocated to Jones, Alabama where they began their family.

While residing with my aunt in Sylacauga, Alabama, I was a member of the Harper Spring Baptist Church. As a young man, regardless of what took place on Sunday evening, I would find myself in church on Sunday morning. Since becoming a Christian at an early age, this has been my practice.

Chapter Two

UNITED STATES MILITARY

"The Steps of a Good Man are ordered by The Lord."

B eing the second of eight children, (four boys and four girls) was not easy; however, there was always love in the home. We all worked on the farm. Of course, there was not much else to do in Jones, Alabama but work on the farm. I was an excellent farm worker. However, God had a greater purpose for my life. After an extended period of time on the farm and fulfilling other responsibilities, on September 4, 1942 I was drafted into the United States Army and reported to Fort Benning, Georgia for duty.

When I reported to Fort Benning, Georgia on September 18, 1942, I determined from the outset that I would be the best soldier in the United States Army. After spending a few weeks in Fort Benning, about 275 of us were transferred to Hampton Road

Embarkation in Newport News, Virginia. On our first day there, the First Sergeant of the company called a formation to give work details and training schedules. He asked if anyone in the formation could type. I held up my hand and he asked me to "fall out," i.e., to dismiss myself from the formation. He took me to the company orderly room and gave me a training schedule to type. He had it all printed out, and by the time he went outside for about fifteen minutes and returned, I had typed the schedule. He then gave me another typing assignment, and the same thing occurred. He picked up the phone and called the battalion sergeant major, Master Sergeant Percy M. Draper, and informed him that I have a "whiz kid" who can type as fast as you can talk. The Sergeant Major came to the company orderly room and observed my typing skills. He then asked, "How would you like to work for me at battalion headquarters?" I said to him, "Sir, I am working here in the orderly room." These are the words he said to me: "I am over the orderly room." And with that he cut orders transferring me from the company orderly room to the battalion headquarters. This was the second day at this new site. I had not drilled one step. I had not been given any other duties, other than to report to headquarters each morning. I never shall forget what Sergeant Draper said to me. "Here is a book of regulations; I want you to study them because I am going to make you my morning report clerk." From that assignment, I began a long career in military administration and personnel management.

Each evening when the other soldiers were either gambling or drinking beer or engaged in some other worldly activities, I was in the headquarters office absorbing army regulations. I had only been at the post one month when I received my first promotion to private first class. One month later, I was promoted to corporal. Two Months later, I was promoted to what was called then "buck sergeant." Three months later, I was promoted to staff sergeant. On July 1, 1943, I was promoted to master sergeant and I was selected to take a group of soldiers to Vancouver Barracks, Washington. From the time I was sworn in at Fort Benning, Georgia to my promotion to master sergeant, the elapsed time was nine months and twenty-seven days.

It may seem that I am bragging, but before I was promoted to master sergeant, I knew regulations backward and forward. I could give the basic regulation on any matter pertaining to the Army.

In December 1943, I was transferred from Vancouver Barracks, Washington to Fort Lewis, Washington to form the Third Quartermaster Unit Training Regiment in preparation for duty in the European Theater of Operation. At that time, at age twenty-one, I was the youngest regimental sergeant major in the entire Armed Forces of approximately seven million men and women, both black and white. The report came out in the *Army Times*. As I stated earlier, I was determined to be the best soldier in the Army. And to be sure, it was not easy, for the military was still segregated. Of approximately 5,000 troops, less than twenty-five were black. It was difficult! But as I look back, God was with me.

In February 1944, I took the 554th Quartermaster Training Battalion to Europe. Our first stop was Glasgow, Scotland, and from there to Birmingham, England; to Cardiff, South Wales; and finally to Barry, South Wales. It was from that point that we prepared to depart for France. We were scheduled to depart D-Day plus twenty. The area in France where we were to disembark was still in enemy hands. Our battalion finally arrived on Normandy Beach, France in late August. We were housed in field tents in an apple orchard in the community of Isigny, France. We were to remain there until October 1944, at which time we relocated to the port in Cherbourg, France. I remained with my unit, the 554th Quartermaster Service Battalion, until November 1945, at which time I was rotated to the United States.

While stationed in Isigny, France, I was sergeant major of a battalion with the responsibility of providing grave registration service, laundry service, food preparation, transportation and other support services for combat troops. There were seventeen quartermaster companies under my battalion. It was at this point that I observed, on a daily basis, truckloads of the bodies of young men who had been killed in front line battles against the Germans. Our task was to provide temporary burial service until these young men could be relocated to permanent burial sites. To see the bodies of young men being wrapped in body bags and dumped on the ground like bags of sand was an experience that I shall always remember. This was not just one day per week; this was a daily routine. It was at this location that I learned of the Black Tank Battalions that had destroyed the city of St. Louis. The White Tank Battalion had not been able to take the city, but after the two Black Tank Battalion were called to take the city, it was accomplished in short order. At this time, the Armed Forces were totally segregated. It was at this location, and I shall never forget this incident, that I read an article in the *Reader's Digest* where the then-Senator Bilbo of Mississippi made the statement that Negro soldiers were not worth more than $50 per month, and that their families were not entitled to any military allotments. Here I was, a young black master sergeant in the United States if America, where one of its elected officials stated that because I was black, I was not entitled to the same compensation that whites, of equal rank, were entitled. But again, this experience prepared me for life. While serving as depot sergeant major at the Port of Cherbourg, France, I experienced injustices to our black soldiers that were unbelievable. As battalion sergeant major, I had the responsibility of publishing promotions and transfer orders for both enlisted men and officers. This, of course, was at the direction of the depot commander. In order for a second lieutenant to be promoted to first lieutenant, it was necessary to remain in a given duty assignment for ninety days. I observed black second lieutenants serve in a position for eighty or eighty-five days, then be assigned to another duty position where he was required to start all over. By the same token, I observed white officers being placed in a position where they remained for ninety or ninety-five days and were promoted to first lieutenant. This was done routinely. Both of these officers may have completed Officers' Candidate School on the same date, received their commission on the same date, and were even sent to Europe on the same date. But often the white officers would be promoted to captain and the black officers still remained in the position of second lieutenant.

In early 1945, I was offered a direct field commission as a second lieutenant. I turned down the offer because of the treatment that the black officers had received. Fortunately, I was a master sergeant and received amenities that the second lieutenants did not receive. While serving as depot sergeant major, I had assigned to me a Jeep driver, maid for my quarters (I lived in a two-bedroom apartment, with kitchenette.), and a personal secretary. Second lieutenants lived in quarters where two or more of them shared the same room. It was terrible. But, I believe these experiences prepared me for what I would confront in later years. On November 5, 1945, I departed from my post in Cherbourg, France to return to the United States.

On November 11, 1945, I was in Brussels, Belgium waiting to embark on the ship for the return to the United States. At 11:00 o'clock that morning, there was an assembly where the National Anthem was played. It was one of the saddest days that I had ever witnessed. Leaving my comrades in Cherbourg, and the many

French friends that I had acquired while there, was overwhelming. My intention was to return to the United States for a thirty-day vacation, re-enlist, and return to Europe. The United States had a policy at the time that not more than six percent of Negro soldiers could remain in Europe. Strange!

I returned to the United States, leaving many of my personal possessions in France with the idea of re-enlisting and returning. To my disappointment and amazement, I was prevented from returning, based solely on my race. I need to state here and now, while it is fresh in my mind, that the then-Supreme Allied Commander, General Dwight David Eisenhower, signed many General Court Martial Orders, condemning black soldiers to death based on testimony from white French women who had testified that they had been raped by Negro soldiers. I was privy to many of these General Court Martial Orders.

On October 31, 1945, I was honorably discharged from the United States Army with the hope of re-enlisting and returning to Europe. After several weeks and a number of calls to the Pentagon seeking to return to Europe, I was informed that the policy in force was that Negro soldiers could not be returned. Even after reporting that many of my personal belongings had been left in Europe, I was still denied the opportunity to return. What was I to do? I had only a few more days remaining that I could re-enlist and retain my same rank as master sergeant. The Army offered no hope. I called the Air Force and was told that if I would report to Fort

Campbell, Kentucky, I could re-enlist in the United States Air Force and retain the rank of master sergeant. So on November 1, 1945, I enlisted in the United States Air Force in the rank of master sergeant. I spent the next seventeen years in the Air Force, retiring with military honors on October 31, 1962 at Griffin Air Force Base in Newburg, New York.

As I look back over my life, it was by design and divine providence that I was inducted into the military service. It gave me the unique opportunity to travel in many parts of the world, interacting with a variety of customs and cultures and, at the same time, finding my own identity in life. During my twenty-plus years as a military career man, I was privileged to serve in Scotland, England, South Wales, France, Belgium, the Philippines, Okinawa, Japan, Korea, China, Africa, and Spain. I can only thank God for this opportunity.

During my military stay overseas and in the States, I studied at the University of Maryland (Heidelberg, Germany Division); the Armed Forces Institute, Madison, Wisconsin (Tokyo Division), and the Far Eastern University, Manila, the Philippines. As part of my religious studies, I did extended studies with the Moody Bible Institute of Chicago, Illinois for eight consecutive years, as well as the Northeastern Bible Institute of Essex Falls, New Jersey. I received a Graduate of Theology Degree from the Detroit Baptist Seminary in 1967, and was later awarded an honorary Doctorate of Divinity Degree from the Detroit Baptist Seminary. "I had fainted, unless I had believed to see the goodness of the LORD in the land of the living." (**Psalm** 27:13)

While serving in Japan from June 1950 until September 1952, I was assigned to the 1808th Airways and Air Communication Service Wing in Tokyo, Japan, where I served as command historian and public information specialist. In this assignment I earned the Air Force Commendation Medal for distinguished service. It was my responsibility to compile historical reports on the activities of our units from Hawaii to Korea, in addition to writing news reports and radio announcements for the wing commander. It was a challenging experience that required discipline and determination. I am a better person today because of this exposure.

I think one of the unique experiences of my military career occurred when President Harry S. Truman signed an executive order desegregating the Armed Forces in 1949. For the first time in my military career, I was placed in charge of white servicemen. President Truman stated in his executive order that for those individuals who did not desire to serve with Negro troops, they could depart from the military with honorable discharge. Very few left the military, although it was difficult for many of them to serve under Negro leaders.

I remember in 1950, I attended the Armed Forces Recruiting School in San Antonio, Texas, for nine weeks of intensive training as an Air Force recruiting salesman. There were approximately 200 individuals in the class, from lieutenant colonels to airmen first class. Of that number, approximately fifteen were black military persons, and only one or two of them were master sergeants; I was one of them. It was difficult for all of us. During the graduation exercise, I was required to give a ten-minute speech. In the public speaking class, out of 200 students, I graduated number one in the class.

In October 1952, I returned from Tokyo, Japan and was assigned to duty at Mitchell Air Force Base, near Hempstead, New York, as chief clerk of the Advertising and Publicity Division of the 1806th Air Force Recruiting Group at Mitchell Air Force Base. It was at this location that my life began an upward spiral. I had returned from Tokyo as a young man, and ready to settle down. For the first two or three months at this location, I kept a low profile, spending time getting acquainted with the surroundings in the New York Metropolitan Area, and of course, learning more about my responsibility as sergeant major of the recruiting group at that base.

It was in early January 1953, that I met a young lady who would become my future bride. It was an unusual happening, for I had reached a stage in my life where I was ready to settle down and began to live as a responsible man; not that I was not responsible before, but I really was focused on the future. This young lady, who would eventually become my wife, visited the Air Base one evening with a young airman and his wife. They came to the recreation room where I was playing a game of pool. The young man, by the name of Sylvester Jackson, was an airman first class and was a record clerk who worked in my office. When they entered the recreation room, I looked up and spied the young lady who had accompanied them, and the first thought that came to my mind was, "Uh! That Is Going To Be My Wife."

I continued to play pool, and a few days later, I asked my clerk to ask this young lady if I could call her. Her reply was, "What does he want to call me for?" A few days later, I made the same request and received the same answer. I was persistent and asked the third time, adding that I just wanted to visit her. She gave in and I visited her the first week in February 1953. From the very first visit, I was convinced that this young lady would eventually be my wife. I visited her every evening and on February 27, 1953, I made a statement to the effect, "I want to ask you a question and please do not say no." She asked me to explain, but I said to her, "Just say yes." Recalling that evening, I suspected that she felt that I would get "fresh" with her. But after an extended period of silence, she asked again, "What is it?" I said to her, "Just say yes." Finally, she said, "Yes." Then I asked this question, "Will you marry me?" It seemed that she jumped two feet off the floor. She then paused for an extended period of time and finally asked, "When?" I said, "March 21st." She then asked the question, "Why March 21st?" I responded, "Because it is the first day of spring." After another period of time that seemed an eternity, she responded by saying, "Yes." I responded, "I will be here tomorrow and we will go for the rings."

On March 21, 1953, I united in holy wedlock to Miss Willie Mae Bates of Hempstead, New York. To this union, six children were born: Wanda Karen, Helen Marie, Joyce Ann, David Kevin, Daniel Kerwin, and Dorothy Jean. After spending thirty-four years together, Willie Mae passed into eternity in the early morning of June 17, 1987.

The story does not end here. In 1954, I was assigned to an Air Force recruiting group at Mitchell Air Force Base as chief clerk of the Advertising and Publicity Division. I held this position for four years. I was a member of the Antioch Baptist Church, licensed to preach the Gospel, and I had just married a wife. All this reminds me of the parable in Scripture, where God gave each of his Servants ten talents to occupy until His return. I could not make excuses, there was work to complete. I was sure that I would stay in the States, but God said, not yet.

This letter from the *late* Reverend Andrew Bennett was written on my behalf, but God's purpose and plan for my life was still incomplete.

Director of Military Personnel, Headquarters, USAF:

"Dear Sir: I am writing this concerning Sergeant Parker who, I understand, has been chosen to go abroad for duty in the near future. We are hopeful that some plan can be worked out whereby he can remain at his present post. Sergeant Parker is a "model citizen"

of this community and is very active in religious work. As Assistant Pastor of the Antioch Baptist Church, he is a conscientious, zealous, and energetic Christian worker. He is truly an inspiration to our membership of approximately 375 members, and especially to the young adult members. I find him to be the most valuable and sincere assistant that I have known. Sergeant Parker has been considered for Ordination. I hope to have him appear before the Ordination Council later in this year or during the early part of next year. I earnestly and prayerfully hope that nothing will intervene which will require the cancellation of these plans, as he has worked so faithfully to prepare himself for this important occasion. As a Minister, he has made excellent progress since receiving his license a year ago; primarily, because he has had the opportunity to exercise his Gift. It would be unfortunate for him were he placed in a position that would deprive him of the opportunity for continued development and growth through the medium of practice, and individual group counsel. It is doubtful if these broad avenues of support would be open to him overseas. I am respectfully requesting that every consideration be given to allow him to remain at his present station. Andrew Bennett, Pastor."

As much as I wanted to stay at my post, and as much as I appreciated the generous letter from my pastor, Reverend Bennett, God said, "Not yet, the assignment is not complete, finish the work."

Nevertheless, in October 1958, I was again sent overseas to Ben Guerir Air Base in Morocco, North Africa, where I served as station manager, program director, and detachment commander for an Armed Forces radio and television station at that base. It was a station that operated twenty-four hours per day, for six-and-a-half days per week. It was the only English-speaking radio station within a radius of 200 miles. This station was location at the foot of the Atlas Mountains and just a short distance from the Sahara Desert. I was not upset for having to return overseas; I took each assignment with determination and sincerity. I determined to complete each job given to me to the best of my ability. I knew that the Lord was preparing me for a greater purpose. I say to you, "Wait on the LORD: be of good courage, and He shall strength thine heart: wait, I say on the LORD." (**Psalm 27:14**) "And let us not be weary in well doing: for in due season we shall reap, if we faint not. (**Galatian 6:9**)

OFFICE OF THE BASE CHAPLAIN

HQ 3926TH COMBAT SUPPORT SP., USAF

APO 113, NEW YORK

SUBJECT: Letter of Appreciation and Commendation, MSGT H. David Parker

Ben Guerri A.B. Morocco, Africa

25 October 1958 –

"During the past eight months, I have been at Ben Guerir Air Base, Morocco, Africa, as Base Chaplain. It has been a very real privilege and pleasure to observe the effective impact which can be made on a Base by a non-commissioned officer of integrity, Christian courage, and ability. I refer to Master Sergeant H. David Parker, who, during the past year, has been NCOIC in charge of our Radio AFRS, Teacher of our adult Bible Class, an Usher in our Base Chapel, Leader in Sports and Cultural activities on the Base, and has proven himself one of the most popular and effective non-commissioned officers here.

Under his leadership, our Adult Bible Class grew steadily and rapidly from a very small group to its present size of more than 30 enrolled, with a normal attendance of nearly that number. Many men and women have had their lives strengthened by his forthright Christian leadership and teaching.

As a Senior Non-Commissioned Officer, MSgt Parker has demonstrated a manly loyalty to God and an unswerving devotion to the highest principle of decency and honor.

45

Sgt. Parker has a fine sense of humor, attractive personality; maintains good health with an ever-buoyant attitude toward life at its best. He is a good organizer and speaker; has done an excellent job with maintaining Radio AFRS at a high peak of efficiency and positive influence of its high caliber program. He is completely sincere, conscientious and capable. This is a very much finer Base because of his presence and influence. I wish it were possible to be honestly able to give such commendations to all men of our USAF, but Sgt. Parker is an unusual and valued member of our Air Force to an unusual degree. I whole-heartedly recommend consideration for his promotion which may expand his opportunity for such leadership."

Ben Jackson
CH (Maj) USAF
Base Chaplain

Yes, I repeat, while in the military, I gained an abundance of experience. My duties in the Armed Services took me to many countries, namely: Scotland, England, South Wales, France, Belgium, the Philippines, Okinawa, Korea, Taiwan, Formosa and Morocco, North Africa. I received numerous awards and military decorations for service: Army Commendation Medal, Good Conduct

Medal with one silver loop, American Campaign Medal, European African, Middle Eastern Campaign Medal with one bronze service star, World War II Victory Medal, Army of Occupation Medal (Japan), National Defense Service Medal, Air Force Longevity Service Award with four bronze oak leaf clusters, United Nations Service Medal, and the Korean Service Medal. All of this was accomplished by the grace of God. I take no credit for my accomplishments; it was the gracious and mighty hand of God. At the age of twenty-one when I was drafted into the military, I promised to give it my best.

God was leading me in the path of self-sufficiency and righteousness. I kept my head on straight, did not follow the lead of others, and was determined to trust the Almighty God. It was He who kept me day by day.

In October 1959, I finally returned to the United States and was again assigned to Mitchell Air Force Base as the assistant editor for the base newspaper. I continued my duties at the Antioch Baptist Church, happy to be home with my wife and family, and of course my church family. On May 6, 1961, I was assigned to an Air Force reserve wing in New York City as an information technician and an Air Force field inspector. I traveled to and from this assignment on the Long Island Railroad. My travel to New York City was finally over:

THE ROUTE OF THE DASHING COMMUTER!

THE RETIREMENT ROUTE – YOUR TICKET TO THE GOLDEN YEARS

Your Dashing Days Are Over: The Commuter's Race you've won.

We'll Miss You On Your Usual Train.

But We Hope you'll Be Having Fun!

In grateful acknowledgment of your years as a faithful

commuter in fair weather and foul

Be it known from Manhattan to Montauk and

from Greenpoint to Greenport

(Change at Jamaica) that

H. David Parker

On this, the 31st day of October, 1962

Has achieved the coveted status of

Commuter Emeritus

On the Long Island Rail Road

Happy Retirement – Thomas Goodfellow

I retired with military honors on October 31, 1962, after serving in the Armed Forces for more than twenty years. The assignment was completed.

Trust in the Lord with all thine heart; and lean not unto thine own understanding. **In** all thy ways acknowledge him, and he shall direct thy paths. **(Proverbs 3:5, 6)**

Chapter Three

EMANUEL BAPTIST CHURCH

God with Us
"In thee, O Lord, do I put my trust; let me never be ashamed…" (Psalm 31:1a)

I had been called as pastor of the Emanuel Baptist Church of Elmont, New York. By the grace and mercy of God, I was licensed to preach the gospel at the Antioch Baptist Church of Hempstead in 1957, and was ordained as the assistant pastor of Antioch on December 9, 1960. This was the first time in the history of churches that one was ordained as assistant pastor (not assistant to the pastor) of a church. I served for three years under the leadership of the late Reverend Andrew Bennett before accepting the call to Emanuel. On February 17, 1963, I was installed as Emanuel's fifth pastor. Incidentally, I had just retired from the United States Air Force in October 1962.

The order of service for the installation program was as such: The special selection was "Without God I Could Do Nothing." Now, that is a fact in my life's service. The installation service began at 3:30 o'clock. Reverend Andrew Bennett, my former pastor, of the Antioch Baptist Church of Hempstead, preached the sermon; his congregation and choirs accompanied him. The post-installation services for the week, February 18th – February 22nd included the following pastors: Reverend Charles Neal, Faith Baptist Church of Hempstead: Reverend Morgan M. Days, Shiloh Baptist Church of Rockville Centre; Reverend Clinton C. Boone, Union Baptist Church of Hempstead; Reverend Stanley Hines, First Baptist Church of Westbury. When I looked at the church bulletin for that Sunday morning, February 17, 1963, I knew that there was much work to be done; much teaching and encouraging. The financial statement for the previous Sunday, February 10, 1963 was listed as follows: Sunday School $6.76; Missionary Offering $14.13; Morning Service $122.32; Evening Service $12.62. The grand total for the day was $155.83. If I had been called just to receive a high salary, or for recognition, I perhaps would have been tempted to leave after six months. But, the Lord called me to preach the Gospel of Jesus Christ, in the hedges and highways, and He would give the increase. I came to Emanuel with a servant's heart. I was asked by one of the seniors in the community, "Son, why did you come here?" My reply was, "The Lord sent me here."

The 23rd Psalm is my testimony: "The LORD is my shepherd; I shall not want. He maketh me to lie down in green pastures: he leadeth me beside still waters. He restoreth me soul: he leadeth me in the paths of righteousness for his name's sake. Yea, though I walk through the valley of the shadow of death, I will fear no evil; for thou are with me; thy rod and thy staff they comfort me. Thou preparest a table before me in the presence of mine enemies: thou anointest my head with oil: my cup runneth over. Surely goodness and mercy shall follow me all the days of my life: and I will dwell in the house of the LORD forever."

I know, without hesitation, that I was called by God, and during my first eighteen months as pastor, 126 persons were added to the membership of the church, which led me to organize the following auxiliaries (ministries): The Adult Choir, Senior and Junior Usher Boards, Junior Choir, Nurses Unit, Laymen's League, the H.D. Parker Intermediate Chorus, Young Matron's Missionary Circle, and the Senior Choir. During my pastorate, I ordained to the deaconship of Emanuel seventeen deacons. Also licensed/ordained six ministers who were called to lead churches in the metropolitan area: Reverend Horace Allen, East End Baptist Church, Brooklyn; Reverend Willie Belcher, First Baptist Church, Cutchogue; Reverend Charles Ancrum, Antioch and Genesis Baptist Church of Jamaica; Reverend Ronald Simpkins, Freewheel Baptist Church, Jamaica; Reverend Kent Edmondson, Mt. Olive Baptist Church, Oyster Bay, Long Island; Reverend Donald Butler, Community

Baptist Church, Southampton; installed Reverend Reginald Lewis, Liberty Grove Baptist Church, Taylorsville, North Carolina, and licensed to the ministry my son, David K. Parker.

I was led by the Spirit of the Lord to organize the Jamaica Square Improvement League of Elmont. Because of my foresight and concerns for the community, Nassau County and the Town of Hempstead appropriated $1,287,000 for the improvement of streets, curbs, sidewalks, lighting, and drainage in the Jamaica Square area.

During my short pastorate, slightly more than three years, the church was led to purchase new pews and pulpit furniture, new organ and piano, new stained glass windows, and a full air conditioner system. I came to Emanuel with a mind to work, not only on the beautification of the church, but mainly winning souls for Christ. "Crusading is what I do."

The church family consisted of approximately sixty members when I was installed on the third Sunday in February 1963. The Lord added to the church in His own divine power, and the membership grew from sixty to 700 members. I take no credit for the addition. Praising God, and having favor with all the people. And the Lord added to the church daily such as should be saved. (**Acts 2:47**) I know for sure, I love the Lord and I love people, and my purpose is always to please Him. My first message to Emanuel was, **"Give Me An Understanding Heart."** I thank God for guiding us across the years. We made mistakes together, but we also profited together from those mistakes. During the road we travelled, God was our mainstay. Nevertheless, without the superintendence of the Holy Spirit, we could not have achieved the measure of success spiritually, financially, and materially, that we accomplished. We give God the glory!

Due to the rapid growth of Emanuel, the Lord led me to purchase additional property for future expansion. Because of the sacrifice, faithfulness and dedication, year after year, the good Lord just kept on blessing us. In 1972, we purchased a new bus, and a scholarship fund was established to encourage our high school graduates to further their education.

Early in my ministry, my heart was open to the indwelling of the Holy Spirit. The fervent prayer of the righteous availeth much. As the pastor of a congregation, and a minister of the Gospel, I have always viewed my role as "A **father to his children.**" As it relates to young people, I have always made myself available to the youth, to hear their concerns and set what I believe to be a healthy example for them. To be a successful pastor, one must always be approachable. I made it my business to hear the concerns of the people of my congregation, both young and old (mature), to provide whatever support deemed appropriate. I have discovered, and especially in recent years, that many young people do not receive proper parental instructions, training and role modeling. I am convinced that training should begin at a very early age and such training should come from the parents or parent. The training and molding of our children should not be left to our school systems or the church.

As pastor of Emanuel, I taught by example, following the footprints of Christ my Savior. Just a reminder, it is easy to follow a leader when he knows the direction in which he is headed. The young people followed my leadership wholeheartedly; they loved the discipline and training that were given. I believe that young people should be taught, first of all, to respect themselves. I believe that in many circles the idea of spiritual training has been abandoned. At the Emanuel Baptist Church of Elmont, New York, I sought constantly to foster a spiritual atmosphere among the people, old and young, who were committed to my care. I am convinced that when pastors provide the proper spiritual atmosphere, their congregations will respond accordingly. Our young people are involved in a variety of activities other than spiritual, such as scouting, bowling and after school activities.

With a personal relationship with my heavenly Father, I also cherished a personal relationship with my earthly family. I made it my business each Sunday to greet all of the members and friends who attended our services. I greeted them individually; I knew all 700 members by name. You may call it being nosey, but I also knew where most of them worked. I made myself available; my office was always open to the concerns of my sheep. My sheep knew me by name. The members were always comfortable in speaking with me; there was no big me or little you, we were one family; the body of Christ. I was on call 24/7 to glorify His name. My twenty-plus years as a professional military man and my trust and faith in God equipped me for the task. My ministry extended far beyond the church. I made it a habit of going into the schools in the area, to voice my opinion and offer suggestions; my presence was always welcomed by the superintendent, faculty and staff.

I strove to be flexible, but never abandon my spiritual conviction to accommodate anyone. I never compromised the Gospel to gain popularity or recognition. My concern in ministry was always, "At the end of the day, was God pleased with my service?" Honesty, integrity, self-respect, love and compassion should be the hallmark of, not only the pastor, but everyone. As the Golden Rule teaches, "To love thy neighbor as you love thyself."

On October 25, 1987, under my leadership, Emanuel celebrated a tremendous accomplishment with the dedication of the New Emanuel Baptist Church, with a construction cost of $2.8 million. I thank God that He blessed us to erect a house of worship. We never had to beg or sell dinners. We believed in tithes and offerings. The Scripture states, "Bring ye all the tithes into the storehouse, that there may be meat in mine house, and prove me now herewith, saith the Lord of hosts, if I will not open you the windows of heaven, and pour you out a blessing, that there shall not be room enough to receive it." (**Malachi 3:10**) Yes Lord, with God all things are possible.

After my thirty-seventh year as Emanuel's pastor, these comments were recorded in the *Elmont Herald*:

As a member of the Elmont Community Reverend Parker found and organized the Jamaica Square Improvement League, the area's civic voice. Reverend Parker has touched more lives than he could ever imagine, not only through his ministry, but also by his outpouring of genuine love, concern and justice for everyone throughout the world. His actions illustrates how life should be lived as a true Christian soldier. He will go miles to see that one has food and shelter. As the Founder of the Nassau Council of Black Clergy, and during his three-year presidency, he moved welfare families from hotels and motels in Nassau County and placed them in private homes. This resulted in the closing of twelve welfare hotels and motels in Nassau County. In 1979, he was appointed Chairman of Nassau County Interracial Task Force where he dealt with issues of segregation and discrimination in the Nassau County Police Department and other county agencies. It is reported that Reverend Parker is acknowledged throughout the streets of Long Island as the "Archbishop of Long Island." He is recognized for his strength and

diplomacy and quest for justice. Reverend Parker reaches out to bring the Word of the Lord not only to his Elmont community, but also as far away as St. Vincent West Indies, Central America, Jerusalem, Nassau Bahamas, and to Okinawa, Japan. He facilitated the purchase of medical sterilizers, blankets, towels, and other equipment, to assist the people of St. Vincent West Indies to establish a health clinic.
(Recorder by: Cathy Ferrigno)

Moving from the small church, as we called it, to the new church edifice, did not change our heart, attitude, or commitment. I thank God for that significant occasion in my life and prayed that He would continue to shower His blessings upon my ministry. There is yet territory to be conquered and I believe that, as I approach the twilight years in my pastoral ministry, God will permit me to conquer that territory. Boasting is not of God, for the Scripture states, "Except the Lord build the house, they labour in vain that build it..." **(Psalm 127:1)** "Upon this rock I will build my church; and the gates of hell shall not prevail against it (**Matthew 16:18b**)."

Now, I must thank my family for their love, support, devotion, and encouragement which have been the source of my strength in my desire to continue to press forward. I thank my late wife, Willie Mae Parker, of thirty-five years, and my lovely and devoted wife Flora, my children, and my church family who nurtured me in my weakest moments. I thank God for their care and concern. In the name of Jesus, we achieved some noteworthy measures of success, the most important being ministering in such a fashion so as to increase the church membership from sixty to over 700-plus active, participating members. Yes Flora, who is my number one fan and critic, when I get home, I thank you for your invaluable support and encouragement, knowing full well that you will continue to stand by and with me as I seek to achieve higher horizons for God. Your love is unsurpassed and I will cherish it always. **To God Be the Glory!!**

When we survey the path over which we have trodden, we recognize that only a loving and compassionate Savior could have given us the victory and safe passage through the vicissitudes that accompanied these years. In the words of the Psalmist, "O, give thanks unto the Lord, for he is good; for his mercy endureth forever." **(1 Chronicles 16:34)**

Because we serve a God of truth, history was made again at the Emanuel Baptist Church on Saturday, December 1998, when Emanuel's congregation, political leaders, friends and other community leaders gathered to dedicate the new facilities that had been recently completed. The new facilities included day care facilities, nursery, class rooms, a computer training center, new bath rooms, library, and a chapel. The theme for the occasion was "Unto the Glory of God; And for the Uplifting of Humanity." The thought for the occasion was "…How awesome is this place! This is none other but the house of God…" **(Genesis 28:17)**

When a grateful and determined and dedicated people work cooperatively and sacrificially, with faith, and under the banner of an unfailing, ever-conquering God, their labor will always be crowned with success. Lest I forget the sainted dead of bygone days whose voices are hushed in mute silence, we owe a debt of gratitude for their services and sacrifices. I would be remiss not to pay the highest tribute to the officers and members of Emanuel for their unparalleled and unfaltering response to my leadership over the years. Their steadfast determination, coupled with their unblemished confidence in me, gave rise to a personal inspiration that goes far beyond the mere expression of words. **Thank You**!

As stated in Paul's epistle, "For I am not ashamed of the gospel of Christ: for it is the power of God unto salvation to everyone that believeth; to the Jew first, and also to the Greek." **(Romans 1:16)** I take the Gospel of Jesus Christ seriously, and never believed in playing in the pulpit. It is God's sacred altar to challenge and lead His people. The good Lord has been with me all the way and has not withheld His blessings from me. Emanuel, I cannot thank you enough for being with me, following my leadership. Flora, I am counting on you to assist me through all of my undertakings, and especially as I undertake the demanding task of writing my book. With your encouragement and assistance, it shall be done.

As I moved into the twilight years of ministry, thirty, thirty-five, forty and forty-five, Emanuel salutes with these kinds words:

- ➤ Special thanks and Appreciation for **Thirty Years** of Extraordinary Service, Commitment, Love and dedication to the Emanuel Baptist Church. "How Beautiful are the feet of them that preach the Gospel of Peace." (**Romans 10:15**)

- ➤ In recognition of your Leadership as Undershepherd. Feeding the Flock for **Thirty-Five years**. <u>Paraphrased</u> "Feed the flock of God which is among you. Taking the Oversight thereof, and when the Chief Shepherd shall appear, ye shall receive a Crown of Glory that shall not passeth away." (**1 Peter 5: 2a,4**)

- ➤ In recognition of **Forty years** of service. "Let the elders that rule well be counted worthy of double honour, especially they who labour in the word and doctrine. (**1 Timothy 5:17**)

- ➤ In the wake of your **RETIREMENT**, and in recognition and appreciation of **Forty-Five years** of unwavering and visionary leadership of the Emanuel Baptist Church of Elmont, New York, we the Officers and members, as a testimony of our love and Respect, deem it appropriate to confer upon you the honor and title of **PASTOR EMERITUS.** "Therefore, my beloved brethren, be ye steadfast, unmovable, always abounding in the work of the Lord, forasmuch as ye know that your labour is not in vain in the Lord." (**1 Corinthians 15:58) AMEN, AMEN!**

And so it is. When I went to Emanuel, I asked the Lord to give me forty-five years with His people. He honored my request. I recall, as if it were yesterday, when I was called to preach the Gospel of Christ, I was on a ladder that reached from earth to heaven. I looked back at the multitude of people, and GOD said, I will never leave thee nor forsake thee. My God never fails.

I came to Emanuel at the young age of forty-two, with a full head of hair, with vim, vigor and vitality, and I retired at the ripe old age of eighty-seven, still with vim, vigor and vitality. What a mighty God we serve!! "He that dwelleth in the secret place of the most High shall abide under the shadow of the Almighty." **(Psalm 91:1)** I have no regrets, only a heart of thanksgiving. "The days of our years are threescore years and ten; and if by reason of strength they be fourscore years, yet is their strength labour and sorrow; for it is soon cut off, and we fly away." **(Psalm 90:10)**

The time has come, as pre-ordained by Christ our Savior, to relinquish my position as His undershepherd of His beloved people, **The Emanuel Baptist Church of Elmont**! To these wonderful people of God, forty-five years ago, you extended to me the solemn and confident call to become your pastor, shepherd and spiritual leader. for these forty-five years, I did my best to please Christ, my Savior and to live up to His expectations. It was a wonderful and blissful forty-five years!

To all who are reading these words today, my beloved Emanuel, friends across this nation and other regions of this universe, I wish for you God's choicest blessings in all your endeavors, as I make my exit from this region of God's domain. I will never forget the joy that I have experienced on this journey; and especially the engrained joy that I experienced with my co-laborers in Christ. Do not worry about me, I am in the Lord's hand. Forty-five years of pastorate; fifty-eight years of preaching the Gospel! Let me say with absolute certainty, this joy that I have, the world does not know; only God.

Again, special thanks to my lovely and devoted wife, Flora (F.D.); I thank you always for your invaluable support; your encouragement and love. I know that we will continue to walk hand in hand wherever God so leads. And again to my children, Wanda, Helen, Joyce, David, Daniel and Dorothy, you are all grown now; keep the faith. To my "grands" and "great-grands" "Grandpa" has endeavored to set the proper example for all of you. I urge all of you to continue to walk the path of righteousness. "...No man, having put his hand to the plough, and looking back, is fit for the Kingdom of God." (**Luke 9:62**)

The hand of the Lord is yet guiding and directing my path. I am no longer the pastor of Emanuel; I am still a preacher of the Good News of Christ.

On March, 2008, Flo and I relocated to Baltimore, Maryland. We are still on the battlefield for the Lord, telling men and women that the wages of sin is death and the gift of God is eternal life. In our stay here, good news, on April 16, 2011, I celebrated my ninetieth birthday, with friends and colleagues. Is there anything too hard for God? "I have been young, and now am old; yet have I not seen the righteous forsaken, nor his seed begging bread!" **(Psalm 37:25)**

If you are ever in the New York area, I encourage you to drive down Hempstead Turnpike, make a left turn on Reverend H. David Parker Avenue, which leads to the Emanuel Baptist Church. God's Holy Ghost Headquarters.

And now I leave all of you, my readers, with these words: "If in this life only we have hope in Christ, we are of all men most miserable." **(1 Corinthians 15:19)**

A LOOK AT THE CHURCH

"The Last, Best Hope"
(Matthew 5:13-16)

When one observes the state of affairs of our nation, he should have no hesitation about returning to the church as "The Last, Best Hope." It seems that the other manmade methods and modes have failed: Politics, science, education, economics, etc. I hold that the church is "The Last, Best Hope." Where does our responsibility lie? "Ye are the Salt of the earth; Ye are the Light of the World; Ye are the City set on a hill." Therefore, "Let your light so shine before men, that they may see your good works, and glorify your Father, which is in heaven." **(Matthew 5:16)**

The other day I read Austin Sorenson's booklet, which contained these words of wisdom: "the church is not a dormitory for sleep, it is an institution for workers; it is not a rest camp, it is a frontline trench." "It is all right for preacher to comfort the distressed, but it is also the preacher's duty to distress the comfortable."

People who are gripped by the conviction of the biblical admonition, as uttered to the Corinthian church by the Apostle Paul, look beyond this veil of tears and this tabernacle of clay. He said to them, "If in this life only we have hope in Christ, we are of all men most miserable." **(1 Corinthian 15:19)** This suggests that regardless to what transpires in this life, it is only temporary; and a shadow of that which is to come.

65

Here is the obvious fact that we have but one life to live. The question is, "How well are we living it?" Life is short, and each time we meet on Sunday morning in our stained-glass gothic-style sanctuaries, we make history, for we pass this way but once.

If we live to be three score and ten, this means that we have 3,640 weeks in which to live and fulfill our mission and ministry. We need, therefore, to examine ourselves both as individuals and as a church living organism. Such examination might inquire into the following: What things are important to us? What are our goals? What are the principles upon which we function? Where do we place our trust, our hope, and our confidence? What is our relationship with God and to our fellow man? If we look seriously, deeply, and honestly at these questions, we may observe that some drastic surgery is needed in our lives.

While the Church, at its best, is more than an institution, it is, nevertheless, an institution. It has an organization and a structure, but the Church also has a mission and a ministry. One of the most discussed questions in the Church and in the world today is whether the mission and the ministry of the Church in the 21st century is being throttled to death by its structure and organization. In reference to salt and light in our scriptural reading, these two qualities of life are essential to well-being. The mission and ministry of the Church are to be salt and light in the world. If it is true, as some suggest, that the structure and organization of the Church have overshadowed and throttled the ministry and mission of the Church, then the salt has lost its saltiness and the light is hidden under a bushel. In that case, the salt is not salting the world, but only street corners here and there; the light is not lighting the world, but only a few plots of ground. We need to take a look at the setting of our traditional church intuitions.

If the body of Christians known as the Church is to be salt and light of the world, each of us, as members of the body, must take the salt and the light to the world at large; to every nook and corner; every hamlet and region of the world. I am more convinced that this can best be accomplished, not as the Church becomes a power structure by which it can force its pronouncements upon the world; or by which it can influence the world with its institutional weight, but rather as each of us, as members of the Church, becomes a responsible citizen in the world. After all, you and I spend more time in the world than we spend inside the walls of the building.

The question may be asked: "What is God trying to redeem?" Is He trying to redeem a series of institutions in the world, or is He trying to redeem the world? John 3 16 answers the questions: "God so loved the world that he gave his only begotten Son." In Luke Chapter 9, there is an account of the transfiguration experience. Peter wanted to build a tent in which they could stay and enjoy the wonderful experience on the mountaintop, but Jesus took them down the mountain to heal a sick boy.

So, where are the mission and ministry of the Church to be performed? Where is the salt to be? Where is the light to shine? This is to be done, not within the four walls of a building, but outside the walls; in our homes, at our place of business, where we labor with our hands, in our science laboratories, in our places of government, in the public recreation areas, in our schools, on our college campuses, at our club meetings. Jesus said to them, "Go into all the world and preach the gospel to all creation. Whoever believes and is baptized will be saved, but whoever does not believe will be condemned." (Mark 16:15, 16) Matthew 5:16 records, "In the same way, let your light shine before others, that they may see your good deeds and glorify your Father in heaven."

In these places, the salt is to preserve life and to add taste to our existence. In these places, the light is to dispel the darkness and to bring its glory and hope. The sanctuary (inside the building) is the place where the lamp is lit, where it is filled with oil, where its wicks are trimmed. It should never be the place where the lamp is left. It is not a sanctuary lamp, but a street light that the Church represents.

The Christian, then, as a responsible citizen in the world, has an "in" and "out" rhythm of life. He comes "in" to the Church for cleansing, healing, worshipping, learning, and renewing. He goes "out" for salting, lighting, giving, fighting, and saving the world. The gathered people of God, who meet for worship and renewal, must always become the scattered people for service and action.

Yes, "Ye are the Salt of the earth." Yes, "Ye are the Light of the world." Yes, "Ye are a City set on a hill." Salt is to be used wisely.

Light is to be burned. All of which reminds us of the words of Jesus, "For whoever would save his life will lose it, and whoever loses his life for my sake will find it."

What is the last, best hope in this sin-cursed, disturbed world? It is the Church of Jesus Christ. You can anchor your soul in it, for it is the "Old Ship of Zion." Never despair of its failing, for I heard Jesus say one day, "Upon This Rock, I will build my Church, and the gates of Hell shall not prevail against it."

Chapter Four

THE EASTERN BAPTIST ASSOCIATION, INC. OF NEW YORK

Ninth Moderator

1976-1980

48th Annual Session

My Early Relationship and Inaugural Address

56th Annual Session

57th Annual Session

59th Annual

THEME: "Let's Go Eastern"

EBA 48TH ANNUAL SESSION

J uly 1969, the Eastern Baptist Association is in its 48th Annual Session in the Borough of Brooklyn, New York. Three years after being called as pastor of the Emanuel Baptist Church, I have been asked to respond to the welcome address. I take this opportunity to recognize the presiding chairman, Mr. Reed; Moderator James, and the political leader, the Honorable Abe Stark, President of the Borough of Brooklyn; his Honor, Mayor John V. Lindsay, mayor of the great city of New York, and our illustrious State President, Dr. Sandy F. Ray.

After hearing these warm, wonderful, words of welcome, I find myself confronted with the same dilemma as the little black boy who could not remember just what he wanted to be in life. There is a current television commercial in which several black and Puerto Rican youngsters re asked what they want to be in life; A doctor, replies one; a lawyer, replies another; a nurse, a dancer, an airplane pilot, a policeman, a model, a movie star, a judge, a mother, the president. Finally, the television camera pans in on the face of a little lad who is asked the same question. With excitement registering on his face, he searches for an answer, but suddenly realizes that all the choice professions are taken. With a smile f confidence and the true simplicity of a child, he replies: **"I Want**

To Be Something!" So, after being so graciously and warmly welcomed, I am like the little lad: I don't know just what to say, but one thing is sure: "**I Want To Say Something**!"

In my excitement and enthusiasm, however, I must maintain some semblance of brevity. Here, I am reminded of a story I heard about a deacon in a Baptist church. It seems that the pastor appeared in the pulpit on Sunday morning with one of his fingers heavily bandaged. Curiosity got the better part of one of the deacons and compelled him to ask another deacon, "What is wrong with the pastor's hand?" The reply was quick and direct: "I understand that while shaving this morning, he had his mind on his sermon and cut his finger." The other deacon, after a moment of hesitation, said in a somber voice, "It is too bad, but I hope that next Sunday morning when he shaves, he will keep his mind on his finger and cut his sermon!" I pray that it will not be necessary to so categorize me.

Seriously, it is with deep joy that we have listened attentively to these expressions of greetings from the various agencies of this community. (Mayor Lindsay taking time out from his busy schedule; mayor of the greatest city in the world; his television show entitled, "**With Mayor Lindsay**." Today, it is "**Mayor Lindsay With Us**.")

You have welcomed us to Brooklyn, the most populous of the five Boroughs of New York City. With an area of over eighty square miles; and over 200 miles of shoreline; eleven miles long, and from seven to eleven miles wide; ranked fifth in the United States in industrial production... this is Brooklyn, to which you have welcomed us.

You have welcomed us to Brooklyn with its twenty-three sharply defined neighborhoods and cultural lineage. South Brooklyn known as "Little Italy," the major portion of the Jewish population occupying that section known as Brownsville, and the black citizens domiciled in the Bedford-Stuyvesant section. History tells us that the site of Brooklyn originally belonged to the Canarsie Tribe of the Algonquin Indians, the nation which occupied all of Long Island. Brooklyn has a colorful history and renowned reputation. It was named after a small town in Holland called "Breucklen," which means "Marsh Land." Brooklyn does have a beautiful history and continues to make history. Not too long ago, the citizens of Brooklyn had the vision and exercised the wisdom to send to the United States Congress the first black woman in the history of our great republic...in the person pf the Honorable Shirley Chislom.

Brooklyn, for a long time during the past school term, dominated the headlines of our nation's newspapers because of the Ocean Hill-Brownsville situation. And lest I be guilty of gross negligence, I must acknowledge that God has graced Brooklyn with some of the most eminent and able princes of His Church. It is here that the esteemed president of our Empire Baptist Missionary Convention, and vice president of the National Baptist Convention, USA, Inc., in the person of Dr. Sandy F. Ray; and our able and dedicated moderator, Dr. Hylton L. James, conducts the affairs of these ships of state. These men are renowned preachers of righteousness and administrators of meritorious achievements.

This is Brooklyn, and it is here that you have invited us and made us welcome. In considering all of these facts, coupled with the warmth of which we have been received, I am compelled to employ the words of Peter, when he was engulfed in that Transfiguration experience on the mountain with his Lord, and cried out in exultation, "**Lord, it is good for us to be here.**"

It is with a spirit of gratitude, then, that we accept these expressions of greetings from the hearts and lips of this community. We are most happy to be here in your fair city.

We are also grateful to know that you have opened to us the doors of your homes, your hotels and motels; your cafeterias and lunch counters, and your churches. We are especially grateful to the Reverend Mr. Reed for the comfort and conveniences that he and his fine congregation have provided for us. Let me assure you, Reverend Reed, that your facilities and generosity will not be abused.

Finally, we are here, not on a pleasure trip, but on business for the King; the King who has called us from darkness into the marvelous light. Two distinct purposes, I believe, compel our gathering in this 48th Annual Session: First, to report to the people of this great association on the status of our stewardship during the past year, and secondly, demonstrate a continuing loyalty to the Christ who has said, "*I Am The Way,*" and who has redeemed *us by His blood*. We are not here to protest but to preach. We are not here as diplomats, but ambassadors; ambassadors for Christ. We are not interested in bombs but Bibles. We are not here to pry into your affairs, but to practice Christian virtues. We are not here to fight, but to fulfill the task entrusted to us. We preach not a gospel of outer space, but a Gospel of inner grace; not guided missiles, but guided missions; not soils, but souls; not Jets but Jesus.

Ladies and gentleman, it is in this spirit and this setting that we accept these warm expressions of greetings, on the behalf of our moderator, the official family of this association, and the messengers and friends assembled here. I am confident that when this session shall have concluded its deliberations, Brooklyn will be a better place in which to live, work and play...because we were here.

When you return to your homes and to your fields of labor, it is my prayer that you will convey the Good News that the Eastern Baptist Association, under the dynamic and devoted leadership of Moderator Hylton L. James, is still climbing; climbing and reaching for the blessings of that perfect day. Climbing beyond the piercing arrows of a cruel and cynical world; climbing until one day it will reach the presence of Him who awaits to welcome the worker and the faithful with these words: "Well done, thou good and faithful servant: thou hast been faithful over a few things, I will make thee ruler over many things: enter thou into the joy of the Lord." **(Matthew 25:21)**

EBA – EARLY RELATIONSHIP

At this juncture, it is important, at least for me, to catalogue my relationship with the Eastern Baptist Association of New York, Incorporated. I began attending the association shortly after assuming the role as pastor of the Emanuel Baptist Church of Elmont, L.I., New York, in February 1963. Little did I know at that time that I would face future challenges, as I began my journey with that great association.

Several years later, Reverend Mr. Charles Ancrum, senior pastor of the Friendship Baptist Church of Roslyn, Long Island, New York, assumed the role as financial secretary, where he served for several years prior to relinquishing the position. Shortly after he relinquished the position, Reverend Dr. Hylton L. James, Moderator, recommended that I would be appointed to the position. I served in the position for six years, until Dr. James completed his tenure.

It was time to choose a replacement for Dr. James. Someone asked, who would be the best person to succeed him as moderator? Dr. James replied, "Reverend H. David Parker." The question was then asked, "How large is his church and what size is his congregation?" Dr. James replied with vigor that, "It did not make a difference what was the size of the church or congregation," "he knew more about this association that anyone here; and he would be the one that I would recommend." Dr. James further stated that I had served as his financial secretary for a number of years and at each annual session, when I gave my report, it was impeccable, not one penny off. Therefore, he concluded, "He is the man that I highly recommend for the position as moderator of the Eastern Baptist Association.

It is worth noting here that I did not campaign for the position; I did not ask anyone to vote for me. Dr. James appointed a nominating committee to present a candidate and when the committee met in June 1976 at the Mt. Zion Baptist Church in Jamaica, Reverend Dr. John B. Mason, host pastor, there were twenty-seven committee members present to vote and twenty of the twenty-seven recommended that I would be nominated for the position of moderator.

There was one gentleman on the nominating committee who really did not care for me and he stated that it was not right to recommend me for the position and that the committee should go back to the association for clarification. There is always one. Someone stood up and said, "No, it is not necessary to go back to the association. Our purpose for being here is to nominate a person for moderator and we are going to nominate Reverend H. David Parker." After further discussion on the matter, I took the results of those votes and went back to the association and presented the results to the board meeting and I was unanimously elected as the moderator of the association in July 1976.

In preparing for my inaugural address, I made note that the new theme for the association would be, <u>Let's Go Eastern</u>." When I took over the association, the body consisted of only 132 churches. My first major task after assuming the position of moderator was to elect a cabinet.

When I became moderator, the annual fee for the auxiliaries was $35 and the annual fee for the churches was $50. Shortly after my inauguration, I increased the annual fees for auxiliaries to $50 and for the churches to $100. These increases were necessary because there was an outstanding mortgage on the headquarters building of $102,000. The headquarters building at 275 Kingston Avenue in Brooklyn was purchased under the leadership of Moderator Hylton James, but it was on the verge of being lost due to non-payment to the seller, Mr. Young.

As moderator, I was fortunate to have as my financial secretary, Reverend Ray Perry of the First Baptist Church of Glen Cove. He was an outstanding secretary and kept immaculate records.

I return now to the headquarters building of the association. The day after I was installed, I began going to the headquarters six days per week, from 9:00 a.m. until 4:00 p.m. I still carried out my pastoral duties at the Emanuel Baptist Church, even working many evenings. I maintained an office at the headquarters building. I had a full-time secretary, and we maintained a perfect record of all monies received. I would drive from Nassau County daily and would stop by the church in Elmont; do my work there and then go on to the headquarters in Brooklyn. I received no funds for transportation to and from Nassau County. In fact, when I would give my annual address, I would receive an offering of between $3,000 and $4,000. I never received monies for expenses. My purpose and main goal was to pay off the headquarters building and to leave monies in the account.

The question may be asked, "How did we obtain funds to satisfy our obligations?" The answer: we instituted a fund-raising venue. Each auxiliary would sponsor a monthly luncheon and all funds that came in through such venue were earmarked for liquidating the indebtedness on the headquarters building.

It is important that I mention again that when I assumed the role as moderator, there were two mortgages on the property: One mortgage was with Mr. Cain Young from whom we purchased the building, and one with the National Westminster Bank (Bank of America) of Hempstead. It was my responsibility to ensure that the monthly payments were made according to signed contracts. The second mortgage held by Mr. Cain Young, in the amount of $9,840.81, was satisfied on November 1, 1979.

At this junction, I must pay tribute to one of the outstanding members of the association who assisted me immensely in liquidating the indebtedness on the headquarters building. She was Mrs. Virginia Bull of the First Baptist Church of Bay Shore, Long Island. She was the financial secretary and worked for the Tax Department of the City of New York, where many times we ran short on paying our bills, including our mortgages. I would call Mrs. Bull and explain our situation and she would give us one- or two-week grace period to satisfy our financial obligation. Many times we did not have money to satisfy our obligations to the bank and I would call the bank president and he would give us a two-week grace period. It was a challenge, to say the least. It took a lot of prayer to deal with the people of God in such a great undertaking. Thank God, I was able to meet the challenge. I was blessed to have in my administration an outstanding and dedicated team of workers.

MODERATOR'S INAUGURAL ADDRESS

E lected as the ninth moderator, my inaugural address was given at the Emanuel Baptist Church of Elmont, in July 1976. At this time, and for a specific purpose, our meeting is in obedience to the divine decree of the ever-loving Savior.

To say that the burden of this office does not weigh heavily upon my shoulders, even now, would be a gross misrepresentation of the facts. But I hasten to add, recognizing the awesomeness of the responsibility that I've inherited, that the "Ship of State" (The Eastern Baptist Association) has now passed to a new activist, who must now bring to fruition the dream, hope and aspiration of his predecessor, Dr. Hylton L. James.

Today, I give special recognition to Dr. Johnson, Executive Director, Empire Baptist Missionary Convention; Dr. J.T. Reeder, President, New York State Progressive State Convention; Dr. J.D. Washington, Moderator of the United Missionary Association of New York City. Your presence this evening, and your words of encouragement and pledged support will mean much to me and this administration in the months to come. And to you, Dr. James, it has been a real pleasure to have served in your cabinet during the past six years. I believe that our relationship was always cordial, warm and mutually beneficial. I wish to thank you for the support that you have promised, and I know that I shall not be disappointed in that commitment. *I wish to pause here* and now thank my lovely wife, Willie Mae, for her many years of loyal support and dedicated affection. She has been a true helpmate of the first magnitude. And to my six children, who have always been concerned about "daddy's welfare," and who think that he is the greatest. My thanks to you for being a "Good Bunch." And last, but certainly not least, my humble thanks to a wonderful congregation, the Emanuel Baptist Church Family, who responded to my leadership, and permitted me to grow as God would have me grow. And I know that in my new role as moderator, you will continue to support me; pray for me, and wish me well in this new undertaking and responsibility.

In retrospect, it might be helpful, at this point, to make an historical analysis of what has been termed the greatest Baptist association in America. How and why did she come about? What has she accomplished? What is she doing now? Where does she go from here? Perhaps, all of these questions will not be answered this evening, or next month, or even next year, or ever, because great ideas; meaningful dreams, and superlative goals are seldom realized fully in one's lifetime. Like the artist who paints a landscape in the evening sunset, or the author who composed a score to a heart-throbbing tune, or a poem with great depth, he is never fully satisfied with his work.

But how and why did Eastern come about? Five-and-one-half decades ago, a handful of Baptist witnesses, in the New York Area, with an urge and inward burning desire to be bettered messengers for Him who had called them, decided that there should be an organization of Baptist churches that, by uniting, could better present the message of Jesus Christ, and at the same time, provide an outlet for wholesome, Christian fellowship. Hence, the Eastern Baptist Association was born in 1921. It continued, unabated, to proclaim the message of Jesus Christ, and to fellowship and support the work of the State Convention and other national Baptist bodies and schools.

The Eastern Baptist Association was guided these fifty-five years by renowned men, dedicated and committed to the cause of Jesus Christ. Eastern is unique, for she can boast tonight of five living moderators, whose imprint on the sand of time, and in the hearts of countless thousands, can never be erased. These stalwart Baptist giants, whose faithful and unselfish devotion to duty, nurtured Eastern from its infancy to the present. Most of them have gone home to get their reward, but their works do follow them: Dr. Kimball L. Warren; Dr. W. H. Rasberry; Dr. Porter W. Phillips; Dr. James Bennett Mitchell; Dr. James R. Moore; Dr. Sandy F. Ray; Dr. Benjamin J. Lowry; Dr. Hylton L. James. Of course, I was elected at the 55th Annual Session of this Association on July 16, 1976.

On April 29, 1970, under the leadership of Dr. Hylton L. James, Eastern took title to that piece of property known as 275 Kingston Avenue, Brooklyn, New York, from Mr. Cain Young, owner. The expressed purpose for this bold, courageous, and aggressive action was to provide headquarters building, with facilities for an educational center complex and office space. Today, the original cost of

$205,000 has been reduced to something less than $75,000! Let me pause to state here that Eastern will always be indebted to Dr. James for his vision. He is deserving of our sincere gratitude for having laid the foundation upon which we can and must build for the future.

What is Eastern doing now? Well, frankly, we are at a point of reassessing our position and direction. Our forward progress has been impeded, but we begin now to feel a forward surge. To accelerate the momentum of our forward progress, it will require pushing, pulling and praying on the part of Eastern's total constituency. This cannot and must not be a "one-man operation." We are in this venture together; and we must work together if we are to realize our envisioned success. With the intellectual, spiritual, and financial resources concentrated in the more than 150 churches of Eastern, we are able to conquer any mountain!

I know that this administration will need the support of every pastor, every auxiliary president, and every layman of this association, if we are to achieve our objectives. As your moderator, I am here to listen. But I am also here to be the moderator. And there can only be one moderator at any given time. We are going to have dialogue in this administration, and just as soon as I can synchronize our calendar of events with the various auxiliary presidents, I shall be calling a meeting of the Board of Managers of this association. In this connection, I am asking all auxiliary presidents to meet here, at Emanuel, this Tuesday, at 11:00 a.m. sharp. Please bring your proposed program dates that they may be reconciled with the dates of the parent body. This is necessary to avoid overlapping, and prevent a duplication of efforts.

Where Does Eastern Go From Here? It depends on where Eastern wants to go. And bear in mind, my sisters and brothers, we get all of the success for which we are willing to pay. Success does not come cheaply or without sacrifice. It comes with a high price tag. But if Eastern desires to go higher; Eastern can go higher. Eastern will have to pay the price.

Permit me to re-emphasize, here, that we should not look for an overnight revolutionary upheaval in the administration of this association. We shall move cautiously but progressively. Encourage all of our elected officers to counsel with their predecessors, as much as possible, and I also encourage mutual cooperation and respect in this regard. I am completely satisfied with the members of my cabinet, and feel that we have a good team. There is not one iota of doubt on my part as to whether or not I will be able to work harmoniously with this team. I believe that the elected officers of the auxiliaries are competent, capable, and dedicated. I urge everyone to give them a chance to prove themselves.

I call upon every elected and appointed officer of this association to give his or her best. I urge you to strive for "Excellence." Never be satisfied with second best. And I cannot over-emphasize the importance of the membership of this association to stand behind and support those whom you have elected. And do not criticize them. Do not put stumbling blocks in their way. Try to understand the pressure under which they will be serving. And they WILL be working under pressure, for I shall be calling for the best from all of them.

My military background and discipline dictate that I ask for and expect excellence from everyone in this administration. Sometimes I will become a bit impatient or irritated when I see someone "fumble the ball," or fail to give his/her best. Try to understand me. Try to visualize the end results of our collective effort, as it relates to the achievement of our objective. I am only looking for, and expecting, the best.

Several people have asked me what type of program I would be submitting to the association. They want to know what the association can expect from me. Well, my high hope and ambition now is to bring about a sense of unity, cooperation, and understanding throughout the association. I believe that we are too divided. We are too fragmented and re-actionized. I would hope and pray that all of the Baptist churches in our associational area, who are not already aligned with an association, would consider casting their lot with Eastern. I welcome them, and can assure them that they will be recognized and appreciated here. So if this administration is successful in bringing about unity, cooperation, and understanding, then the program which I present will be of secondary importance.

I know that you are looking to me to lead you progressively and successfully, to present to you a plan and program that will enhance our association, and to achieve its objectives. To the extent of my ability and capability, I pledge myself to that task. As your moderator, I also expect your prayerful support, cooperation and concern. No one person, regardless of how gifted, can successfully lead a body of this magnitude without the wholehearted support and cooperation of those he leads. By your vote, you have given me a mandate, and I pledge not to fail you. And I ask no more or less of you.

As I have stated earlier, you have given me the best cabinet possible; I believe. Men of proven ability; men who have been tried in the arena of public pressure. Men who have been exposed to a variety of challenges. Men who are effective leaders in their own right, as proven by the effective leadership that they have given to their own congregation. I trust them. I have confidence in their ability. I believe that the auxiliaries of this association are also staffed with presidents of proven ability. They are capable, they are concerned, they are dedicated. But like all of us of the parent body, they are serving, for the most part, in new roles, with new responsibilities and new challenges. All of us are still learners, but willing learners; and as such, we are given to errors. Mistakes and errors are common to us mortals. We are still fallible, all of us, and we recognize this fact. And so when we do err, whether by word or deed, please do not judge us harshly, but show justice, mercy, equity and love. We will certainly be trying; give us a chance!

So what do I envision as a program for Eastern? The immediate goal is three-fold in nature:

- To pay off the indebtedness on our headquarters building. Make it free and clear of all liens.
- To renovate the building and to restore it to its original appearance and condition.
- To bring an allied educational program to our headquarters building, including a religious educational center and a secular tutorial program.

This goal is easily attainable, if we would work together and support the program as envisioned and presented by the moderator. It can be achieved; it must be achieved.

I have personally assigned some priorities for myself. Permit me to share them with you at this time. As far as I am concerned, my first loyalty and allegiance is to Jesus Christ, my Lord and my Redeemer. (Incidentally, this was my position long before President Nominee, Jimmy Carter, made a similar statement about his religious conviction.) So Christ comes first in my life. Secondly, Sister Willie Mae Parker and our six children occupy the second spot in my life. Thirdly, and rightfully so, the Emanuel Baptist Church Family, a most loyal and dedicated congregation, one that has tolerated me and subscribed to my leadership for almost fourteen years, holds that unique third place spot in my life. And finally, the fourth spot goes to Eastern! My wife and children, and the Emanuel Congregation, will be ever concerned about my success as the chief executive of Eastern. Therefore, they will assign the same loyalty, allegiance, and priorities, as I have stated.

Since I have outlined our immediate objectives, the next logical question is: How do we achieve them? Permit me to state, succinctly, what I conceive as the most effective method to accomplish our objective. Listen!

"If each church of this association, under the leadership of its pastor will designate one Sunday per month as "Aid to Eastern," our objective could be realized in short order. For example, the members of the Emanuel Congregation have been asked, and they have responded to give a liberal, free-will after-offering each first Sunday as "Aid to Eastern." They have responded with marked enthusiasm! I believe that many members of our congregation, if not most of them, are more than willing to respond to an appeal of this type. If they know that such a sacrifice is going toward the fulfillment of a worthwhile goal. I hope and pray that each pastor of our association will permit his members to express themselves in this manner. i am also requesting the auxiliary presidents to make a similar appeal to their members."

As pastors and preachers of the Gospel of Jesus Christ, we are custodians of God's most precious resources, "His Creatures." We must learn to serve them wisely. The ancient sage, King Solomon, said almost 1,000 years B.C., that "Where there is no vision, the people perish." (Proverbs 29:18) Those words are just as true and appropriate today as they were when first spoken. Pastors, as shepherds, have the care of the flock committed to them by Jesus Christ, and sanctioned by His divine successor, the Holy Spirit. We must ever be concerned about the whole man. Not only must we take into account his spiritual needs, but his educational, economic, employment, human rights, and housing needs. As modern-day prophets, we must make our appeal for cooperation, sacrifice and concern on the basis of God's inspired Word. For I heard Jesus say one day, "I was a hungered, and ye gave me no meat; I was thirsty, and ye gave me no drink,; I was a stranger, and ye took me not in; naked, and ye clothed me not; sick, and in prison, and ye visited me not." Here, then, Jesus demonstrated concern for the "whole man." The man that must live and exists in a society of modern-day Pharaohs and corrupt Caesars, needs the care and concern of Christ's under-shepherds.

My friends, with the purchasing power of the blacks in our associational area, we should be getting a larger slice of the economic pie. In our communities, we pay for services that we never enjoy. Prophets and preachers, we must address ourselves to these injustices. We must address ourselves, forthrightly, to the housing and

employment plight of our people. Our communities have deterio-
rated to such an extent that many are no longer suitable for human
habitation. We must never cease to fight for decent housing for our
people who are consigned to the lowest economic ladder. As long
as a large segment of our sisters and brothers are "ghettoized," we
must not rest contented, regardless to the status or station that we
have achieved in life. We must learn to use our leverage (vote and
economic muscle) to ensure that our people receive their just proportion of management jobs.

In a few days, we will be going to the polls to cast our ballot; to
express our choice for the President of these United States. Friends,
these are critical, crucial, agonizing times, and we must seek the
guidance of the Holy Spirit, so that when we are asked, "Is there
any word?" we will have what we believe to be the right answer.
This year, more than at any other time in recent history, our people
must be given directions. Are we satisfied with the affairs of this
nation? Will we continue to sit by while the rich get richer and the
poor get poorer, without any verbal or other meaningful protest?
Like the prophet of old, we should tell our political leaders that we
are not the cause of the problems of our society; they are to blame!

Just this past Wednesday, September 29th, the President of these
United States, for the fifty-ninth time, used the prerogatives of his
office, and vetoed a $56.6 billion aid bill. Affected by this veto, if
not overridden, are funds for labor, health, education, and welfare.
I need not tell you who will suffer the most from this insensitive

action. How many more vetoes can the poor people and minorities of this nation endure? During World War II, following the Japanese surprise attack on Pearl Harbor, America produced a patriotic song, entitled, "Let's Remember Pearl Harbor." And when and wherever this song was sung, it had the effect of moving people to their greatest war-production potential. And so I say to you tonight, when you go to the polls on November 2nd, "Let's All Remember The Vetoes."

My friends, I want to close now, but permit me to share some final thoughts with you on this historical occasion. I wish to reiterate here that the office to which I have been elected and installed was not one sought by me. By your vote, however, you have given me a mandate, and I have no choice but to give the office my best. I did not campaign for the office, nor did I ask anyone to vote for me; I have not made any promises to anyone. And so I am free and unencumbered, and can minister the office of the moderator without fear or favor. Concomitant with this position, I do not shrink from the awesome responsibilities that accompany my new position. For I still believe God's Word, "I can do all things through Christ, which strengthened me."

On the night of the election, when the reign of leadership of this great body was passed from Hylton Lancaster James to H. David Parker, these words invaded my heart with resounding clarity, "Lord, Give Me An Understanding Heart!" I had prayed this prayer many times before, but it took on a different meaning that Friday evening at the Berean Baptist Church of Brooklyn, when by your vote, the honor and the responsibility of Eastern, as its chief executive, was thrusted upon me. As I sat there, I recounted and rehearsed the words of Solomon. You know the story. It goes that Solomon had completed his building project for God and had gone to Gibeon, a small village town just six miles north of Jerusalem, to worship. There he offered 1,000 burnt offerings on the altar of God. While at Gibeon, God rocked him to sleep one evening, because He wanted to speak with him, He allowed Solomon to dream, and in the secret chambers of that dream, in the midnight hour, God said to Solomon, "Ask What I Shall Give Thee." Solomon made his request, after recounting the favors that God had already shown his father, David. Then Solomon made this request. He said, "O Lord My God, thou hast made thy servant King instead of David, my Father: and I am but a little child: I know not how to go out or come in. And thy servant is in the midst of thy people whom thou hast chosen, a great people, which cannot be numbered nor counted for multitude. Give therefore thy servant an understanding heart; to judge thy people that I may discern between good and bad: for ho is able to judge this thy so great a people." (1 Kings 3:7-9) This shall always be my prayer: "Lord Give Me An Understanding Heart!"

At the risk of violating the rules of homiletics, I move to another area in this unfolding, closing drama. Since the election in July, and the opportunity to speak with many friends and well-wishers, other thoughts have invaded my mind; chiefly, the words uttered by Caleb, as he spoke with Joshua in Gilgal, concerning his possession of land that had been decreed earlier by Moses, Joshua's predecessor. In the twelfth verse of the fourteenth chapter that bears Joshua's name, Caleb made his request to Joshua. Observe his words, as he builds an invincible case, to substantiate his request. He said to Joshua: "Forty years old was I when Moses, the servant of the Lord, sent me from Kadesh-Barnea to espy out the land; and I brought him word again as it was in mine heart. Nevertheless, my brethren that went up with me made the heart of the people melt; but I wholly followed the Lord my God. And Moses swore on that day, saying, 'Surely the land whereon thy feet have trodden shall be thine inheritance, and thy children's forever, because thou hast wholly followed the Lord my God.' And now behold, the Lord hath kept me alive, as He said, these forty and five years, even since the Lord spoke this word unto Moses, while the children of Israel wandered in the wilderness: and now, lo, I am this day four score and five years old (85) years. As yet, I am as strong this day as I was in the day that Moses sent me: as my strength then was, even so is my strength now; for war, both to go out, and to come in." And now, we visit the Word of the Lord.

"GIVE ME THIS MOUNTAIN"

SERMON–JOSHUA 14

H ere's the Word: "Now therefore give me this mountain, whereof the Lord spake in that day; for thou hearest in that day how the Anakims were, there, and that the cities were great and fenced: If so be the Lord will be with me, that I shall be able to drive them out, as the Lord said." (Joshua 14:12)

And so I say tonight, as Caleb said, as I assume this responsibility, "Give Me This Mountain." It is man's nature and tendency to see the easy way out. It was not so with Caleb, who sought a difficult task. "GIVE ME THIS MOUNTAIN." Mountains offer both advantages and disadvantages. For it is from the mountain top that one can see the approaching enemy. It is from the mountain top that one can breathe the sweet fragrance of God's eternal blessings. Mountains hold varied fascinations. Here things are required to conquer mountains: <u>OXYGEN</u>, <u>ENERGY</u>, AND <u>ENTHUSIASM</u>. As we recount the story, twelve spies went out from Kadesh-Barnea, seventy miles to Hebron, to spy out the land. After forty days of observation, they returned to make their report to Moses. The majority report was filled with negative content. It was dismal; doubtful and discouraging. "We can never possess the land," they said. "The inhabitants eat up each other; they make us look like grasshoppers to themselves; and even in our own eyes, we look like grasshoppers. They project themselves as giants." But the minority report, rendered by Joshua and Caleb, was encouraging and filled with hope. "Yes, there are giants in the mountains; but let us not be afraid or dismayed; God will give us this land. Let us go up and possess it." With their encouraging report, they were able to still the people, and proceeded to rally support.

In the process, and later, Joshua had to take over from aging Moses. Moses having led the children from under the iron hand of injustice, where he was in view of the Promised Land, was taken by the hand of God and led up to Mount Nebo's summit, where he was kissed to sleep, and his body buried somewhere in the soil of that majestic country. God then commissioned Joshua to lead the children to the Promised Land. They had to go over the Jordan. Let me remind you, my friends, that prosperity and success are always beyond Jordan. Out of an original group of more than 600,000 men, besides women and children, only Joshua and Caleb remained alive. Others had died in the wilderness. It was at this point in Joshua's life that he said to the children of Israel, "Choose ye this day whom ye will serve, but as for me and my house, we will serve the Lord." **(Joshua 24:15)**

Caleb, under the supervision of Joshua, now makes his famous request: "Give Me This Mountain." Give me this hill country of Hebron, rejected by others. Give me these giants to fight; give me these problems to solve; give me this land to be conquered; obstacles to overcome; this mountain to climb, and hill to be moved. "Give Me This Mountain."

I wish time would permit me to deal with some historical mountain experiences in totality. For example, I would tell you about Abraham on Mount Moriah; offering his son, Isaac, as a sacrifice. I would tell you about Moses receiving the law, the Ten Commandments, on Mount Sinai, written on tablets of stone, by the eternal fingers of an omnipotent God. I would recount for you the victorious experience of Elijah with Ahab on Mount Carmel. These are all great experiences. And now we see Caleb asking for a mountain; a mountain filled with giants, to be conquered, so that his people, the people of God, could enjoy the Promised Land. But after success in each of these cases, including Caleb on Mount Hebron, there was still another mountain to be conquered.

In the early morning of God's creation, when He said, "Let there be light; and let us make man," the Holy Spirit looked through the telescope of time, and saw another mountain looming in the distance. It was a great, imposing mountain; a mountain called "CALVARY' that would one day come up in the path of man, as he sought to get back to God. He saw obstacles that would prevent him from enjoying the Promised Land. He saw the giants. He saw the persecutions and misunderstandings.

In that difficult situation, Jesus, my Father's Son, steps to the forefront of time, with eternity wrapped in His bosom, and said to His Father, "Give Me This Mountain." Give Abraham Mount Moriah, but give me Calvary. Give Moses Mount Sinai, but give me Calvary. Give Elijah Mount Carmel, but give me Calvary.

Give Caleb Mount Hebron, but give me Calvary. I will go out and fight these giants that are in the hill. I will meet death on half-way grounds; I will satisfy justice. Give me this difficult task. I will conquer death, hell and the grave; so that man can enjoy Canaan.

This man, Jesus, took on Human form, came through forty-two generations, born of a virgin, travelled the dusty, mundane shores of a cruel world; humiliated, despised, rejected and, finally, came face to face with that mountain – Mount Calvary.

Early one Friday morning, my sin-bearer, after a night of abuse and humiliation, took that Roman cross and started up Mount Calvary. Where're you going, Jesus? I am going to Golgotha; I am going to Calvary. After the agony of Calvary, He left the region of the dead. Where are you going, Jesus? You have called your sheep by name; You've led them into green pastures and by still waters; You have guided and protected them; You have died for them. Where are You going now? I hear Him answer, "Other sheep I have that are not of this fold, who have not heard my voice" (John 10:16) I must preach to them; saints in prison: Abraham, Isaac, Jacob, they died in the faith, but have not heard My voice; them I must also bring with Me."

The devil and death called a council with the grave. The devil said, "He baffled my skull in the wilderness of temptation. He knocked me out in the third round on an empty stomach when He said to me, 'man shall not live by bread alone.' (Luke 4:4). But I've got Him now; I will put the handcuffs of hell on His wrists. I will hold Him fast." Death said, "He took several bodies from my clutches, like old man Lazarus of Bethany, but I have put my hands around his neck, now, and cut the silver cord into, and broke the golden bow. He will never escape me now." The grave said, "He unlocked my eternal door and let some prisoners out, and they walked all over Jerusalem one Friday afternoon, but I'll hold Him fast now." But soon that Sunday morning, death had to unloose the grip, and the grave had to unlock her doors and let the "Good Shepherd" live again. The devil had to surrender and be tied to the Master's chariot wheels and let the Master ride out of death into life. I heard Him say, "All Power Is Given To Me In Heaven and In Earth."

Goodbye, Calvary! Goodbye, Grave! Goodbye, Pilate! Goodbye, Judas! Goodbye, Peter!

I HAVE CONQUERED Calvary – "Give Me This Mountain"

EBA – 56TH ANNUAL SESSION

✝

After one year as moderator, I now prepare to give my First Annual Address. The 56th Annual Session is being held at the Shiloh Baptist Church, Rockville Centre, New York.

I come tonight to give you a report of my stewardship for the past year; where we were at this time last year; where we are now; and where we hope to be at this time next year. Whatever successes that we've achieved, we give God the credit, the honor, and the praise. I must quickly add, however, that it has been a year of learning….learning about you and learning about me. It has been an exciting year; a year of challenges; a year of opportunities; a year of disappointments; and, yes; a year that was sometimes shrouded with frustration. But, I thank God for the lessons learned. It has been a real honor and privilege to have been given the opportunity to serve Eastern in the role of moderator during this past year.

Before enumerating some specifics, it would be a breach of supreme ingratitude if I failed to acknowledge the support and genuine concern exemplified by the Emanuel Baptist Church family. I was given unlimited reign to administer the affairs of Eastern. The members gave of themselves in service, and they gave of themselves in their resources, to ensure that I had a successful year as moderator

On July 16th, 362 days ago, at its 55th Annual Session, this association honored me by elevating me to the position of moderator. Thus, I became the ninth moderator in the fifty-five-year-history of this association. On October 1, 1976, at the Emanuel Baptist Church of Elmont, I was officially installed in the office of moderator. That was 285 days ago, and I propose now to give you an accounting of my stewardship for these first 285 days.

Time does not permit me to detail all of our activities for this year. But I shall try to highlight those activities that I consider most important, that will give you a <u>factual</u> account of my stewardship. If I were to tell you that we have made overwhelming progress, and that I am completely satisfied with our achievement, this would be misleading. It would be unfair to you; and a misrepresentation on my part to do so. But despite what you may have heard in recent weeks about this administration – pro or con – I am convinced that we've enjoyed far more 'pluses' than 'minuses.' Let the record speak for itself.

As it relates to my own cabinet, I think that we enjoyed, for the most part, a harmonious relationship. My Vice Moderator-at-Large, Timothy Mitchell, has always apprised me of his whereabouts, and offered to assist me when and wherever I required him. Dr. Lundy, Vice Moderator of Kings; Dr. Jarvis, Vice Moderator of Queens; Dr. Ellis, Vice Moderator of Nassau; and Reverend Tann, Vice Moderator of Suffolk, have all demonstrated keen interest in the affairs of Eastern. They would concur with me in this assessment:

"We could have achieved our goal, if; if; if; we had received the support from our member churches that this administration sought." Our secretaries, Dr. Middleton, corresponding; Reverend Norris, recording; Dr. A.B. Harris, financial, have all demonstrated outstanding ability in the performance of their responsibilities; sometimes under trying circumstances. Knowing the difficulty encountered in maintaining an accurate financial report, I can sympathize with Dr. Harris in his responsibility for preparing his first report. But he has done an outstanding job. Dr. Middleton has kept you apprised of our meetings; his letters have been filled with appeals that should have moved any concerned pastor to action. And Reverend Norris has maintained the minutes of this association that are worthy of emulation by any progressive, forward-looking organization. My personal thanks to all of you.

During this year, I have enjoyed the most loyal support and cooperation from the auxiliary presidents of this association. As I stated in my inaugural address last year, all of us...for the most part...came to our respective positions as beginners. If you were privileged to hear their annual addresses during this session, you will realize that they have been about their Father's business.

I am more concerned now than ever, after observing our association for the past year, that no one can be an effective moderator of this association by proxy or by operating from remote control. Anyone who occupies this seat must touch the lives of the people. He, himself, must be touchable. He must go to the people. He must make the sacrifice of time, talent and his resources. Nothing less will do. If one is looking for prestige, or popularity, or a life of ease, he'd better look elsewhere than that of being the moderator of the largest association in these United States. If his only concern is to seek honor for himself; and if he is satisfied with the status quo, i.e., the marking of time and striving to be the "good guy," then he may be justified in seeking the post. But, this is not a position for a man who has no convictions. It is not a role for one who can be easily swayed by friends, acquaintances, and associates. It is not a position where one can function progressively and escape criticism; however, one is needed who can bear the scorn and ridicule of his peers as well as others.

WHAT WE FOUND; WHAT WE DID; WHERE TO FROM HERE:

As you may recall, when I was inaugurated last October, I used some very curt words to describe my method of operation. Those words still stand. I vowed then that I would learn all that I could about Eastern. I have. I promised to be the best moderator that I could possibly be; I have striven to be so. Whether or not I have succeeded, I leave to your evaluation.

I would be the first person to admit that perhaps, I have functioned in a fashion that would seem foreign to many of you. It has been alleged that this administration has been a "One-Man Operation." I am sure that most people of this association with whom I have worked and had occasion to seek their counsel would refute this allegation. All of us who have ever served in leadership roles, whether earned or had thrust upon us, know that there are certain inherited prerogatives that go with leadership; that these cannot be abandoned, delegated, nor left to others to execute. And so, it has been in this light that I have striven to lead this association. Permit me to say this: a good quarterback will resort to the 'quarterback sneak,' when he feels that to do so will result in a touchdown for his team. Perhaps some of my actions have been of the "One-Man Operation" type. But, I choose to call it just a "quarterback sneak."

You will recall that in my inaugural address, I outlined three specific goals for Eastern: (1) To pay off the indebtedness on our headquarters building; make it free and clear of all liens. (2) To renovate the building and restore it to its original condition. (3) To bring to the headquarters building an allied educational program, including a secular, tutorial program. It is our contention that had this suggestion been followed by the majority of our churches, all of our goals could have been realized by December 31, 1976.

Since this idea did not succeed, your moderator has had to resort to other means of meeting our obligations. I organized the "Moderators' Boosters Committee" last November, and this committee has been an overwhelming success in terms of raising finance for Eastern. Two musicals were held: At Hempstead High School in Hempstead on May 27, 1977–$962.00; At Headquarters Building on June 25, 1977–$232.03. This committee has supported the moderator wholeheartedly. The Ministers' Wives undertook a special project to provide new drapes, curtains, and blinds for the lower auditorium of our headquarters building. This project was temporarily suspended. We're asking the Ministers' Wives to please proceed now, full speed ahead on this project.

Upon officially assuming the role as moderator last October, I sought, immediately, to learn all that I could about its status. There had been much previous discussion about the real estate, water, and sewer tax due on the property. Upon my visit to the municipal building in Brooklyn, I discovered that not only had our property been restored to the tax roll, but there were water and sewer taxes dating back to 1974 that had not been paid. The total tax owed was slightly less than $9,000. I also discovered that our property was on the verge of being placed "In Rem," i.e., put up for auction. This required my immediate and personal attention. Rather than alarm the association, I personally contacted the tax department to ascertain the procedure to follow to prevent our property from going into "Rem." I was informed that the sum of $2,688 would be required by March 23, 1977, which amounted to one-fourth of the total amount due. A special board of managers meeting was called. The sum of $1,800 was realized from this meeting. On March 23rd, I made another visit to the tax department, where I spoke with Mrs. Williams, chief of the "In Rem" section. She informed me that since the bank, holder of our first mortgage, had made tax payment on our behalf, the amount would only be $1,442. This amount was paid and arrangements made to make periodic payments until all back taxes were paid. This action taken prevented our property from being put up for sale.

In consultation with our attorney, who provided legal service in connection with the extension on our second mortgage with Mr. Young, I was informed by him that the deeds to our property were faulty. In searching the records of the property, he discovered that the Eastern Baptist Association was incorporated in 1929. The Secretary of State dissolved the corporation on October 15, 1952, as he had not been able to contact any responsible official of Eastern to determine whether or not the association was still active. The deeds dated April 29, 1970, conveyed to Eastern by Mr. Young, were issued, in fact, to a non-existent corporation. At the time of purchase, there was no Eastern Baptist Association, legally, insofar as the Secretary of State was concerned. In order to avoid future difficulty with respect to disposing of the property, our attorney advised that we should obtain a "confirmatory" deed from Mr. Young. Your moderator approached Mr. Young, who willingly provided a "confirmatory" deed. Eastern now has a proper and bona fide deed, which has been filed and recorded at Brooklyn's municipal building. The original deed is in the possession of your moderator.

So what are the positive aspects of our first year's administration?

- Our tax problem with the City of New York was corrected, which prevented our property from being auctioned.

- A "confirmatory" deed was obtained; we now have a clear deed and title to our property.

- A completely new roof was installed on our headquarters building. Interior renovation was begun in the lower auditorium and offices.

- The headquarters building is now open five days per week, with a full-time secretary on staff. The moderator spends from three to five hours each day, Monday through Friday, at headquarters, administering the affairs of Eastern.

- We have realized increased support from churches that were not previous supporters of Eastern.

- We have been successful in encouraging "some" pastors to render services at headquarters, to expose their congregations to the activities of Eastern. We hope that this practice will continue, and be intensified.

- The Moderator's Boosters' Committee has been formed into a standing committee, and charged with the responsibility of sponsoring at least one fund-raising affair each month. This will take place in the various locations of our association.

- Plans are almost complete to begin a Bible study course at headquarters in late September, or not later than mid-October. But before this can be achieved, there must be additional renovation to the interior of our building. We intend to pursue this goal with renewed vigor.

When we assumed the leadership role of this association last October, we had high hopes and ambition that we could accomplish great things. With more than 150 registered churches, we were certain that we could achieve certain worthwhile and meaningful goals. That belief has not been negated, despite the fact that many of our churches gave only minimal support. Every opportunity that we've had to speak before our association, we have dwelt on the fact that Eastern should own something for herself. During this year, I have attended and spoken at scores of banquets and luncheons. And in every instance, we have had to use the "other man's" facilities. It's about time Eastern would own its own banquet and luncheon facilities. To pay off the indebtedness of our headquarters building, and to bring to this building a viable program, would give Eastern the stimulus needed to do whatever Eastern chooses to do. But we can never achieve any worthwhile goal if we permit ourselves to become embroiled in petty jealousies, strife, contention and the inordinate desire for holding office. One of the things that has impeded the progress of our people has been the dis-unity that so often creeps into our ranks. Let us be honest with ourselves. All of us do not think alike. We do not operate alike. Our methods and modes of leadership are diverse. Everyone cannot be the leader of the same organization at the same time. But I can say to you this evening that I am committed to the task of unifying our people wherever possible. But more than that, I am committed to progress. We have not accomplished this year what we could have, had we followed just some of the ideas advanced by your moderator. For example, we appealed to our churches in February to make a one-time, $500 sacrificial donation, to be turned in at our Pre-Associational Drive. Less than ten churches responded! The question must come to mind, "Do we really want progress?"

In spite of the fact that we did not accomplish all that we set out to do, I have done my best to be a good steward of the resources committed to me. I have made some errors in judgment, perhaps. Because of the urgency of some actions that had to be taken, perhaps, I did not consult with as many people as some would think that I should have. But when a man is drowning, you don't take the time to ask him why he didn't learn to swim, you throw him a life jacket, or something to hold on to. This has been my approach; and, I believe it was the only way, at the time, to rescue our association. I have no regrets for my action.

I have enjoyed this year. I have met some of the finest people one could have the pleasure of knowing; both clergy and laity. It would be untrue were I to tell you this evening that all of them have been that way. I have had some surprises. I have been disappointed; I have even been hurt by some I trusted. But I have learned. I have learned as much about "us" since last October, as I have in all of my previous Christian experience. I can better understand now why our progress, as a race...and especially as Christians...has been so slow. But I am committed to continue my fight until there is a realization of unity and success among us Easternites. But some changes will be necessary, and success is within our grasp.

Here is where your association stands today in terms of its financial obligations. There is a balance due on the first mortgage of only $28,991.25. Our second mortgage with Mr. Young has been reduced to $31,065.60. It is a must that this mortgage is paid; the interest rate on this mortgage is 12 percent. And finally, there remain back real estate taxes, water taxes, and sewer taxes totaling $4,829.20. My friends, I want you to know that there is an aggregate total of only $64,886.05 on our property! We can liquidate this obligation, in short order, if we choose to do so. Let us rise to the challenge. Let each pastor say to himself and to God, we must not permit these obligations to linger any longer. Had my predecessor received the kind of support to which he was entitled, he could have paid off these mortgages in the first five years of his administration. But you know and I know that he did not get the support that he sought and deserved. I pray that you will not treat me as you did him. We, together, can do it. We, together, can be the kind of association that will bring credit, dignity and honor to its people, but it takes "A Conquering Faith." And this brings me to our theme for this session.

A CONQUERING FAITH:

(Numbers 13:30)

There **Is A Word!** Permit me, now, for the next few moments, to share with you some thoughts on our theme, "A Conquering Faith." To set the stage, I would like to give you some scriptural foundation:

"And Caleb stilled the people before Moses, and said, 'Let us go up at once, and possess it; for we are well able to overcome it. But the men that went up with him said, We be not able to go up against the people; for they are stronger than we. And they brought up an evil report of the land which they had searched unto the children of Israel, saying, 'The land, through which we have gone to search it, is a land that eateth up the inhabitants thereof; and all the people that we saw in it are men of a great stature. And there we saw the giants, the sons of Anak, which come of the giants: and we were in our own sight as grasshoppers, and so we were in their sight." (**Numbers 13:30-33**). We could very well talk about "Grasshoppers and Giants," but we shall strive to stay with our theme.

When I consider the evil report brought up by the majority, who were privileged to search out the land, I must reflect on the difficulty that Nehemiah experienced in the rebuilding of the wall. He encountered three adversaries who were determined to discourage him in his effort to rebuild the wall. By name, these critics were: Sanballat, the Horonite. Tobiah, the Ammonite. And Geshem, the

Arabian. Nehemiah was doing a superb job, but according to scripture, he was severely criticized.

The scripture declares, "Now Tobiah, the Ammonite, was by him, and he said, Even that which they build, if a fox go up, he shall break down their stone wall." (**Nehemiah 4:3**) After several unsuccessful attempts to discourage Nehemiah; even an act of conspiracy to assassinate him in the villages in the plain of Ono, Nehemiah gave his critics his famous reply, "…I am doing a great work, so that I cannot come down: why should the work cease, whilst I leave it, and come down to you?" (**Nehemiah 6:3**) I think I can say without fear of contradiction, "Eastern has too many Sanballats on board."

Permit me to say that this association is flush with critics, standing on the sideline, gloating over what they believe to be failures on the part of those who are striving desperately to move this association forward. I have said before, and it bears repeating, that we have the manpower; we have the resources; we have the intellect; and we have the leadership to do whatever needs to get done in Eastern. You may ask, then, why has it not been done; or why is it not being done? The answer is simple: Jealousy/Envy/Strife/Contention/Suspicion/Distrust/Maliciousness. My sisters and brothers, this is our problem. We are our own worst enemy. This association needs more "Doers" and less "Doubters."

The text declares that Caleb stilled the people and said to them. "Let us go up at once, to possess it; for we are well able to overcome

112

it." This was a true demonstration of "A Conquering Faith." We're able; I say to you this evening!

Since the beginning of creation, God has been choosing men for special tasks. It is not unrealistic to take time out...to look back...to evaluate the path over which we have come...and to contemplate the path that lies ahead. We've come this far by faith... and God delights in faith...He honors faith; and especially, "A Conquering Faith."

In the words of our text, we see faith exemplified. Great cities... high walls...tall, huge, ferocious giants are exciting to weaklings. But there never was a city too great, nor walls too high...nor giants too strong that a man of God...possessed with "A Conquering Faith," could not conquer. Faith brings God into every difficult situation and circumstance. The words of our text warm my heart... they fire my ambition...they stimulate my faith. Sight alone can do small things...but it takes faith to conquer that which seems impossible.

I want to serve notice on us this evening that the true Church is a faith business. People of great faith and unselfish ambition are needed in the church today. There is no room in the church, there is no room in this association, for a weakling, faithless, fearful, doubting, uncommitted person. Unbelief is prevalent in many secular areas today, but it has no place in the Church of Jesus Christ.

My friends, as I have said previously, God has always conditioned leaders for His work. He called and commissioned Moses to lead the children of Israel from under the iron hand of Pharaoh. He informed Nicodemus that he was totally unfit for kingdom service, apart from the New Birth. He equipped Paul, on the Damascus Road, for the task of preaching the Gospel of Grace to a Gentile world. So, God has always prepared someone...somewhere... somehow...to carry out His program.

We have made some noteworthy achievements during this past year...and for these we are grateful. But if we have to move out... and on...and up, we must turn our eyes to the unfinished task. We must not allow ourselves to become blindfolded by petty indifferences and faithlessness, which will surely obscure our visions of the unoccupied fields before us. Often times, God's leaders fall short of their goals when opposition and discouragement become their lot. Many will retreat to safe positions, and never realize God-given...God-set goals. What they need is an infusion of that faith that conquers.

In our story this evening, we have two men, Caleb and Joshua, representing the minority's viewpoint. Joshua, on a previous occasion, had discovered that he needed a conquering faith. Though his achievement had been noteworthy, and he was advancing in age, God made it plain to him that his work was not complete. Both Caleb and Joshua were ripe with experience, and God had built up in them a great faith. "There remaineth yet much land to be possessed." God is saying to Joshua, in effect, there are yet 'unclaimed dividends' awaiting you. Joshua and Caleb were cheerleaders in a dark and stormy period. They were animating personalities. I am afraid that too often; we who boast of being children of God, in comparison to Caleb and Joshua, are only faithless dwarfs. Think of it; Joshua was now an old man, eighty-five years of age, having served with Moses for forty years, and now for the past seven years had occupied a major place in the conquest, had subdued and conquered thirty-one kings and their lands, but here he is possessed with a sense of incompleteness. It braces me...I am encouraged, I am motivated when I look at this old man, Joshua...militant, faithful, forward-looking, but ready to listen to God's fresh orders: "Joshua, I know that you are old; I know that you are tired; I know that you've become discouraged sometimes; I know that you've been leading a disgruntled and disobedient people, but there is much land YET to be possessed."

Somehow, we must get the proper perspective of God's work and God's way. We need a new birth hour in our association. God said that Caleb had another spirit. At eighty-five, he was a mountain climber, for I hear him say, "Give Me This Mountain." Eighty-five years of age, yet standing at the base of the mountain, saying "give" it to me. With tremendous argument, with remarkable clearness, with great forecast, Joshua and Caleb summoned their countrymen to make far-reaching decisions. I see in their argument Mutual Action: "Let us go." Prompt Action: "Let us go up at once." Confident Action: "Let us go up at once and possess it, for we are well able." Faith was their chief asset, and God their strong ally.

Listen to the majority's report. They said, "…we be not able to go up against the people; for they are stronger than we." (**Numbers 13:31**) And they brought up an evil report of the land which they had searched…saying, "The land, through which we have gone to search it, is a land that eateth up the inhabitants thereof; and all the people that we saw in it are men of great stature. And there we saw the giants, the sons of Anak, which come of the giants: and we were in our own sight as grasshoppers, and so we were in their sight." This does not sound like men on a mission for God. I ask you this evening, what will you be – Giant or Grasshopper?

Permit me to emphasize, on this occasion, the characteristics of the grasshopper. I believe it to be appropriate to Eastern. The grasshopper is a stubborn creature. He never plans nor prepares for tomorrow, nor for winter. In early summer, he can be seen as a healthy, robust creature. He eats grass all summer, and hops from place to place in tranquil splendor. But he never thinks that one day, "Old Man Winter" will appear. So when that first cold breeze comes in early fall, he is the most pitiful of all the winged species of the field. Too weak to hop and has not prepared for winter! How sad! Friends, winter will come and whether or not you have prepared for it, you must meet winter. In the case of the grasshopper, nature has no choice but to consign him to an early death. What about us? God needs men and women in this program who will stand tall like giants. Men and women who do not look upon themselves as grasshoppers, who can and will say with resolute determination, "We Can Do It!"

In our story here, Moses and the children of Israel had pitched their tents in the wilderness of Paran, having left Hazelroth, where God had cursed Miriam for questioning Moses' authority. In Paran, God said to Moses, "Send men that they may search the land of Canaan, which I give to the children of Israel. Of every tribe, select a man who is a ruler." Moses obeyed God and employed the true democratic method. He selected a man from each tribe – twelve men. His instructions were clear and specific: Listen.

Get up this way into the mountain; see the land, what it is; the people that dwell therein; whether they be weak or strong; few or many. Look at the land, whether good or bad; the cities where they dwell in, whether tents or strongholds; the land, whether fat or lean, whether there is wood therein or not. And be of good courage, and bring of the fruit of the land.

Twelve went to the mountain. They spent forty days and then returned to make their report. Ten came back with discouraging reports. Here's what they said: "It is a good land, flowing with milk and honey; here is some of the fruit. But the people are strong that dwell in the land. And the cities are walled and great; and not only that, but we saw the children of Anak. The land to which you sent us is a land that eateth up the inhabitants…and there we saw the giants, the sons of Anak, and we were in our own sight as grasshoppers, and so we were in their sight." Oh, how discouraging. But listen to the minority report compiled by Joshua and Caleb, and presented by Caleb. His report was encouraging. Listen: "And Caleb stilled the people before Moses, and said, Let us go up at once, and possess it; for we are well able to overcome it." (**Numbers 13:30**) I say to you this evening, be not afraid of the giants out there. We are not grasshoppers, we are men! We're giants when God is on our side. Men of God, and destined for His work. And not only that, God is on our side. And if God be for us, who can be against us?

We need that faith that sees the sunrise at midnight. That faith that sees hope in the midst of despair. That faith that sees doors opened without keys. That's what we need. And I tell you what we must do...my friends...let us stand firm as did Nehemiah when he was severely criticized and ridiculed. Let us stand tall and look Sanballat in the face and tell him, "We are doing a good work and we cannot stop." Let us tell Tobiah, we will never turn back; and finally, tell Geshem, the Arabian, that God's on our side; and we must continue our work. Oh yes, we will be criticized often; many times we will feel like throwing in the towel, and saying, "What is the use?" But stop! When this feeling begins to overwhelm you, think of the words of Caleb: "We are well able!" My friends, let us not fail in our effort. I tell you what we need to do. Let us recapture that spirit of Jerusalem...not when the walls were being built... but when the power of the Holy Ghost fell on the day of Pentecost.

"And, behold, I send the promise of my Father upon you: but tarry ye in the city of Jerusalem, until ye be endued with power from on high." (**Luke 24:49**)

Have you been to Jerusalem? Have you tarried? Have you been baptized? Have you been filled with the Holy Ghost? Well, when this happens, you'll be possessed with a "Conquering Faith." What about it, Daniel? What about it, Shadrach, Meshach, and Abednego? What about it, David? Well, since there is no verbal response from these stalwarts of the faith – let me give you my answer...

EBA – 57TH ANNUAL SESSION

✝

"Let's Go Eastern"–"Let Us Continue To Build." July 13th, 1978, the Eastern Baptist Association is in its 57th Annual Session. We are meeting at the Mt. Sinai Baptist Church, Brooklyn, New York, where the Reverend W. Lymon Lowe is Host Pastor.

By the benevolent grace of our Creator and Savior, we are here in another annual session of this great association. The omnipotent and eternal Jehovah has summoned us to the Borough of Brooklyn, a city with its many-faceted activities and interests, coupled with its own unique history and peculiarities. Nestled in the shadow of the famed Verrazano Bridge, and separated from the great Garden State by the circuitous and wandering Hudson River, with its incomparable shipping port, Brooklyn provides an ideal setting for this 57th Annual Session. It is here that we have come this week to be about our Father's business. It is here, as moderator, that I give my second Annual Address.

I must take a moment to express my sincere thanks to Dr. Russ Williams for his warm and charitable words of introduction and presentation. I express my personal thanks to those of Eastern, to Dr. and Mrs. Lowe, and the entire Mt. Sinai family for being such gracious and charming hosts during our stay here this week.

I come tonight, for the second consecutive year, to report on my stewardship as your moderator. When you shall hear my report, you make the decision as to whether or not I have been a good steward. At the outset, I thank the Eastern family for permitting me to serve as your moderator during the past two years, and especially the past year. It has been a year of learning. We have not by any mean, achieved all that we had set out to achieve. We can say, without fear of contradiction, that we have done our best. The path has been strewn with bumpy and, sometime, unhappy experiences, but by the grace of God, we have continued to move forward. Whatever success that we have achieved, we give God the credit, glory, and the honor. We can say now as we did last year, it has been an exciting year. A year of challenges; a year of opportunities; a year of disappointments; and yes, in some instances, a year that was sometimes shrouded in frustration.

It is an unhappy fact of our times that Christians today are too often faced with contrary winds from all directions; winds that lead to separation and divisions among themselves. In the face of world crises, the Christian Church too often stands with her life enfeebled, her witnesses weakened, her messages, in some measure, discredited by her own differences and dissensions. We see evidence of separation and division on every hand. It is obvious to the discerning eye that the energies which, as Christians, we devote to controversy and conflict, should be devoted to the one great purpose for which Christ exists... "to bring the whole world to the knowledge and fellowship of Christ Jesus."

The duplication of efforts, competition and rivalry among Christians are worse than the waste of resources, serious as this may be. They are a spectacle which lessens the faith of men, brings religions into disrepute, and does daily hurt to the cause of Christ. Amid the controversies of the Church, men cannot grasp the great central message which she should proclaim. The fact which they see clearly is that, however the division among Christians may be, they conflict with the Church's own teachings and contradict her own principles. They know that whatever else the Church stands for, she must; if she truly represents Christ, stand for harmony, for fellowship, and unity, not separation and division.

A careful analysis and assessment of facts will convince any discerning mind that there are too many voices. As a people, as a race, we must learn to initiate actions rather than to always react to actions initiated by others. We seem, most often, to be crisis-oriented. We develop little or no strategy in time of peace, so, when a crisis situation arises, we react hastily and ineffectively. We will never be able to deal with external problems and conflicts, until we are able to solve our internal problems and conflicts. We spend far too much energy and time venting our vengeances on each other. Love should always be the overriding concern of all of us. "Lord, give us the desire to see opportunities to build up rather than tear down," is my prayer.

My honest opinion and confession is this: I believe that the power once vested in the Church, to deal with moral and social problems, has been seriously eroded. When one considers the Borough of Brooklyn, Kings County, we see a colossal structure of church-related organizations, conferences, fellowships, committees, and boards, all purposing to speak for the betterment of a given constituency. We have associations, and conventions, and other organizations based here in Brooklyn. Permit me to pose these questions: What is the overriding, long-term value of these organizations for the betterment of our people? Is there a duplication of effort? Are there specific goals to which all of these organizations can address themselves? Have we permitted splinter groups and dissident elements to rob us of the unity so desperately needed among our people? Have these unhealthy conditions come about because of the inordinate desire of some to head an organization? Is this craving for leadership and recognition destroying our effectiveness? Are too many of us infected with the disease of "officitis" or "leadershipitis?" Have we reached that point in our history where we reject the time-worn axiom, "Where There Is Unity, There Is Strength"? Think on these things!

Last year, as we observed our 56th Annual Session, the Borough of Brooklyn was thrown into chaos during the "Great Blackout." Many sections of Brooklyn still bear the scars of that infamous event. Again, this year, as we meet in this beautiful historic borough, bigotry and hatred reign, tension is high, distrust, anger and frustration characterize the atmosphere. Man stands across the invisible line of uncertainty, peering at his fellowman with distrust, just waiting. He is waiting to see if someone has the answer for his agonizing plight. There is a need for religious leaders of every persuasion to sit down at the bargaining table of brotherly love, not to seek to outwit one another, but to seek earnestly for solutions to their perplexing problem. God must be the head of all of our efforts this week, and the weeks to come. I am afraid that for too long, God has been left out of too many of our decisions. Before we make hasty, irrational statements and actions, we need to know if there is any Word from the Lord. We need to be much in prayer, not only during these times of tension, but consistent; constantly, every day, without ceasing. I solicit the prayers of every believer of this association.

Frankly speaking, at this point, there is not one person in the Eastern Baptist Association who has given as much of his time, his resources, and his energy as your present moderator. I do not apologize nor complain about this; this is the way it should be. I must admit, we have not achieved those desirable and attainable goals that we should have; and, there is a reason for this. We all remember the program that I outlined in my inaugural address, two years ago, and repeated in my annual message last year. However, we failed to achieve these goals; we have made some notable progress. It may be tainted with skepticism, but Eastern is blessed with the intellect, the know-how, the financial resources, the fortitude, and the moral fiber to undertake any venture and succeed. I must admit, and I stand to be challenged and criticized for my position, that Eastern is lacking in UNITY, COOPERATION, and UNDERSTANDING. I think the last three years will bear out this contention. My brothers and sisters, we must be big enough, and courageous enough, to admit our shortcomings, and to criticize ourselves when the need arises. For it is only when we follow this course of action, that corrective and remedial steps can be undertaken.

As we meet here this evening, may we offer a unified prayer that God will give us the Unity, the Cooperation, and the Understanding so vitally needed for our present struggle. Easter is a unique vehicle by which great things can be accomplished to the glory of God, and for the benefit of His people. But, there must be some deep soul searching and new approaches if these goals are to be realized. Our headquarters building at 275 Kingston Avenue was a bold and aggressive undertaking by our esteemed Moderator, Reverend Hylton L. James, who led Eastern to undertake this noble venture. It depicted vision, and insight, and progressive leadership on his part. And to him, Eastern must be eternally grateful.

Having shared some of the negatives of our past years' experiences, let us move quickly to some of those most desirable elements. I should begin by reflecting on the support that I have received from my cabinet: Officers, auxiliary presidents, and pastors in general, and our secretarial staff. Dr. Middleton's letters, announcing drives and special meetings, have been of such clarity and persuasive appeal as to move the most recalcitrant individual to act. No one who has heard the minutes from our recording secretary, Reverend Charles Norris, could have any reason to criticize their accuracy, content, and clarity. He has been a scribe of the first magnitude. Reverend A.B. Harris, our financial secretary deserves the highest praise for maintaining a flawless account of the financial status of our association. Thanks to our Treasurer, Reverend R.D. Brown. We benefited from his wisdom in the area of finance; and he has monitored the proceedings to ensure that all actions were sound and constitutionally proper. It was he who suggested, administered, and brought to a successful conclusion the "Million Dollar Wedding Project."

Finally, special recognition and thanks to the chairman of our Board of Trustees, Reverend Richard Hunter. He came aboard at a time when stability and concern were paramount considerations. He has been an effective fund raiser, and has given the moderator unlimited support and cooperation. He has encouraged his church and many others across our association area to support Eastern's efforts enthusiastically. Lastly, I want to commend Reverend Clinton C. Boone, chairman of the Advisory Committee, for the superb job that he has done with his committee.

I have enjoyed the most loyal support, cooperation, and dedication from our auxiliary presidents. I must thank each of them, personally and publicly, for inviting me to their monthly meetings, and permitting me to articulate Eastern's goals and concerns to their members. As a sideline, I attended so many of the ushers' drives that they made me an "Honorary Marshal." I learned to march; the Ushers' Auxiliary literally put me through the test. You see, when one moves beyond the half-century mark, those hip bones, and knee bones, and ankle bones, just do not respond as in earlier years. And, it did not take me long to discover this fact.

Since our last annual session, your moderator has attended and participated in twenty-seven events in which Eastern was directly involved. Neither time nor space would permit listing all of them in detail. These events have included banquets, luncheons, anniversaries, appreciation services, and weddings. During this year, I have been invited to preach approximately six anniversaries where churches of our association were celebrating their fiftieth year. I was privileged to preach the installation service of several pastors; and the ordination sermon for Reverend E. Burkett of the Greater Jerusalem Baptist Church, Brooklyn, where the Reverend W.F. Folks is pastor. Additionally, I have conducted five revivals for churches of our association.

Permit me, now, to make one or two observations. This year has been rich in experiences for me, as I fore stated. It has been my pleasure to meet and work with some of the finest pastors and lay persons on God's good earth. I am the richer because they permitted me to share in their experiences.

What is the status of Eastern tonight? Where were we two years ago, when this administrated was inaugurated, and where are we today? I will not itemize the contents of our financial obligations; however, I think it is worth noting that in two years, we have reduced our total obligation from $85,853.28 to $48,074.86. Is there anything too hard for God?

We like to believe this to represent considerable progress, during these past two years. Your moderator has always sought to inspire and motivate Eastern's constituency, even when doubt and pessimism were rampant. I will say this evening, as I said last July, I have made some mistakes; to state otherwise would assume omniscience. I am still mortal and mundane. I am sure that anyone sitting here this evening would have made mistakes also, had he walked in my shoes, or sat in my seat. If I had to retrace my course, in all probability I would do things about the same. I think that all of us will agree that no two persons operate the same. Therefore, in my judgement, my method of administering Eastern's affairs was my best way of functioning. One thing that that I can say from my heart, I have done my best.

I see sunlight at the end of the tunnel. Let s hold out and hold together until victory is won. Whatever happens during this annual session, I want this association to know that ever since its leadership was entrusted to me, I have done things to the glory of God. I have not, nor will I ever permit myself to become engaged in trickery, deceit, falsehood, or character assassination in order to be elected to any office. If I am unable to stand on my record of performance and achievement, then I go down! Whatever I have been able to achieve during the past two years, I have done it with honesty and integrity. I believe that those who have worked closely with me will bear me out in this contention.

Your moderator is recommending that a cash effort be made to pay off all indebtedness on our headquarters building within the next six months. The recommendations will include the efforts of every pastor, officer and auxiliary president. For you see, the property at 275 Kingston Avenue, Brooklyn, commonly referred to as "Headquarters Building," was conveyed to Eastern by deed on April 29, 1970. That is more than eight years ago. This is too long for anyone to agonize over a debt that should have been paid off during the administration of my predecessor. Let me hasten to add here that seeking to meet our monthly mortgages, and other obligations, has robbed us of our energies that should have been directed in other areas of vital concern. We had no other alternatives; we had to protect your investment.

Immediately, or prior to the payment of all debts on our building, I recommend that a select committed be appointed to develop a program for the utilization of our headquarters building, acceptable to the majority of the Eastern's constituency, and one that would be beneficial to our total body. This committee, as an alternative, may wish to study the wisdom of retaining this property as a focal point of Eastern's interest. While it is recognized that great and noble endeavors are often met with criticism, doubt and rejection, it is the opinion of your moderator that no building, or other man-made device, should be permitted to destroy the fellowship and love between brethren. Buildings will decay, from the invasion of termites. Gold will canker with time. Flowers will fade and fall away, but brotherly love should be enduring. My sisters and brothers, personally, I would rather have love, fellowship and unity, than to have buildings. But, I believe with prayer, understanding, and cooperation, coupled with the suggested recommendations, we can have all. There is a Word from the Lord:

"Therefore if any man be in Christ, he is a new creature: old things are passed away, behold, all things are become new. And all things are of God, who hath reconciled us to himself by Jesus Christ and hath given to us the ministry of reconciliation; To wit, that God was in Christ, reconciling the world unto himself, not imputing their trespasses unto them; and hath committed unto us the word of reconciliation." (2 **Corinthian 5:17-19**)

EBA – 59TH ANNUAL SESSION

As we meet in the 59th Annual Session of this august body, the Eastern Baptist Association; and as I am privileged, blessed and honored to give my Annual Address for the fourth consecutive year, I must begin by acknowledging the blessings, mercy and presence of a benevolent God through His Son, Jesus Christ; for it is He who has brought us to this significant point in time.

I trust that you will indulge me in these few moments of preliminaries. I extend my deepest thanks and admiration to my side-kick, Dr. Timothy P. Mitchell, for his matchless role of presiding, and for his consistent support given to me during these past four years. He has been an invaluable friend and a source of continuous inspiration. To Dr. and Mrs. Laws, Pastor and First Lady; and the entire Mt. Lebanon family, your selfless and warm hospitality has made our stay here this week one of the most pleasant in recent years. Your support and concern for our comfort and convenience have left an indelible impression on all of us. Your generosity is unmatched and we thank you. To the host pastor, Dr. Bill Jones and the Bethany family, your support and concern in the role of co-hosting this session, have been equally effective. Thanks to you and your fine congregation for this generous support. I know that the entire Eastern family would have me say to you, "Thank you for making the difference." This will go down in the history of Eastern as a week of pleasant memories.

Certainly, I must publicly acknowledge the incomparable support and love that the Emanuel Church family gave its pastor and moderator. This family never faltered, failed, nor complained during these four years.

I should like to give a brief synopsis of the cooperation and support received from my cabinet officers and auxiliary presidents. During these past four years, I have learned the danger of calling names in meetings of this type. I like to feel that the Moderator's Cabinet developed into a smooth, harmonious relationship.

Our secretarial staff; Reverend Norris, Recording; Reverend Tucker, Corresponding, both have done excellent jobs. Dr. Mackey, Chairman of the Board of Trustees; Dr. Jarvis, our Treasurer, and Dr. Boone, Chairman of the Advisory Committee, I am indebted to you for your fine performance and cooperation. I have not the words to adequately commend our auxiliary presidents for your strong and effective leadership: Gertrude Ulmer; Marie Moses; Reverend F. F. Brunswick; Deacon Nathan Neely; and Deacon James Cooley, thank you for jobs well done.

Forty-eight months ago, July 16, 1976, to be exact, by your free and collective expression, you honored me by entrusting to me the leadership of this association. You will recall that Friday evening at the Berean Baptist Church, when Reverend Dr. Hylton L. James invited me to his pulpit for my comments following the election.

My comments were that the reins of leadership had been turned over to a new generation of activists, and that it had become my task to bring the ship into port. Little did I realize then that even though the ship may be within the breakwaters, in sight of the harbor lights, even then one may experience turbulence in what may appear to be calm waters. Thank God, this administration brought the ship safely into port. It is in port now! It is firmly tied up at the pier. As we sought to maneuver the ship to safe harbor, it became necessary, regrettably, to take on new crew members. But I think that what was most important, and I believe that you will agree, is that we are not safely home.

As I make my final report to this august body, I want, first of all, to thank God for sustaining me during the rigors of these four years. And I want to thank you for the confidence that you placed in me, for your prayers, and even for your criticism. You provided me with an exposure that is indeed rare. A special thanks to Mrs. Jarvis and Mrs. McCain for their words of encouragement on Friday evening, July 16, 1976. That evening, both of them said essentially the same thing, at different times: "You will make it; God is With You."

To those aspirants to this position, may I warn you that it is not what one might think it is. Success is not given; it must be earned. This is not a position to seek for honor or prestige. To succeed in this position, one must work and work hard. One must be highly visible. One must be available. One must be cool. One must be able to take criticism; and abuse. One must be available to all the people; the pastor and the pew. Allow me to make this observation; and I hope that you will understand. I now know, by name, at least ninety-five percent of the pastors of this association. I have visited at least seventy-five percent of the churches during my tenure of office. If I can claim any success, it is because I have been concerned about all of the people of Eastern. And I have been there, when needed. I officially opened each and every drive. I express sincere appreciation to those pastors and churches for the lovely manner in which they received us. All of our lives were made the richer because of the outpouring of their affection.

At this point, I praise and thank Eastern for the Testimonial Achievement Banquet, held in my honor, at the beautiful Holiday Inn in Hempstead. I could never live long enough to thank those pastors and lay persons who responded with such an outpouring of love, gifts and words of praise. Thank you, one and all. This was the highlight of my tenure as your moderator, and I shall never forget your love and generosity.

What has this administration achieved during these past four years? Well, when we assumed the moderatorship in July, 1976, there were two outstanding mortgages, totaling $85,853.28, excluding gas, oil, electric bills, and other miscellaneous bills approximating $3,000 additional. All of these debts are now paid in full. The mortgages were burned at the Emanuel Baptist Church, Elmont, on May 16, 1980. Your headquarters building is now an asset rather than a liability. You have a monthly income of $1,500, with the leaser paying all of the utilities. In other words, the $1,500 is clear profit for Eastern.

But where do we go from here, Eastern? Can we be satisfied with the achievements of the past four years? Can we say that we've done enough? The answer must be a resounding NO! As Eastern's motto so eloquently states, "<u>Let Us Continue To Build</u>." May I share some personal concerns as we move into the decade of the eighties? We must not rest on our laurels and yesterday's or yester-year's successes and think that we have done enough. I am afraid that too many of us, even here this evening, are satisfied with just the headquarters building at 275 Kingston Avenue. Well, I am not!

I believe that we need a rallying station; a rallying objective that will be unencumbered by politics or federal or state dollars. We, as a people, can only be free and effective when we chart our own destiny. We cannot chart our own destiny when we rely on others for our survival and substances. Eastern has been given the opportunity to acquire a choice piece of real estate in the Village of Hempstead that would be second to none in New York State for any religious organization. It has banquet facilities for 1,000 persons; twelve large classrooms; a worship auditorium that can accommodate 900 persons; fully air conditioned; a complete gymnasium; six separate bathrooms; parking for 250 cars; a commercial kitchen; three smaller kitchens with dining facilities for smaller groups.

It is located two blocks from the Greyhound Bus Station, and the L. I. Railroad Station; two blocks from two beautiful hotels; two miles from Hofstra University and Nassau Community College; one mile from the beautiful Hempstead Lake State Park, and many other desirable conveniences, such as restaurants and diners are within quick walking distance. To possess this property and properly maintain and utilize it, blacks in this region of the United States could soon be led to achieve political and economic clout that they have never possessed. We could make a difference. We have too long spent our dollars for which we have received no return. I call on all of us to wake up to the reality that we've been duped too long. I venture to say that during my four years in this office, Eastern has spent many thousands of dollars for which we can show nothing but overweight bodies and empty pocketbooks. I, for one, am tired of this backward practice. Under the authority inherent in my position, I shall appoint a committee to survey, investigate, and recommend to this association the appropriate action for acquiring this property. Such committee will be appointed on tomorrow. I should like to think that its first action, when appointed, would be to ascertain what pastors of Eastern will commit themselves to this venture.

Friends, this is an election year; the general election; the Presidential election. Are we prepared to participate in the election process? As I look at the local scene, I think of how Mayor Koch has been continually criticized by the minorities of New York City, and especially the blacks, and rightfully so, for his insensitivity towards the necds of these communities. One thing we, the blacks, must remember: the present mayor is an astute politician.

He may be insensitive to your needs and aspirations, but you may rest assured that he is not insensitive to the ballot...the intelligent use of our vote. And this is where we so often fail. My brothers and sisters, that's the bottom line for blacks in these United States. More than anything else in this country, and especially in the Northeast, we need a massive voter registration, voter education, and most of all, voter participation on the part of our black brothers and sisters. That's the bottom line, I tell you! And until these avenues have been thoroughly traveled, let us cease to criticize or complain about our elected officials. Let's get some voter power and voter savvy in our communities, and when the ineffective politicians fail to serve our best interest, let's vote them out of office. It can be done, but not with rhetoric. It is being done in the South today on a large scale.

The decade of the eighties does not afford us the luxury to dabble in petty jealousies among ourselves. Neither do we enjoy the luxury to trifle in partisan politics. We must embrace that politician, and not political party, that best serves our interest. I urge you to become intelligent Christian voters. Blacks cannot afford to be manipulated this year as in past years. There is too much at stake. Remember that *evil triumphs when good men do nothing*. May I remind us this evening that the two-and-one-half million black men and women in the Metropolitan New York Area make up a powerful and important group of money spenders. In fact, statistics available to me reveal that we spend more than the entire cities of Pittsburgh, San Diego, Baltimore, Miami, Minneapolis–St. Paul, Tampa-St.

Petersburg, Cleveland, Milwaukee, Atlanta, or Cincinnati. Think of this massive buying power!

Friends, on this point, I would make this one simple recommendation: "Let us begin now to chart our own destiny through political and economic achievement." This must become the bottom line in all of our thinking. Let us begin, forthwith, as the Jews have always done, to flex our political power through the intelligent use of our vote. We must no longer permit ourselves to be taken for granted by either of the two major political parties. Votes are power! Let us use them intelligently. In this presidential election year, it is crucial that we become informed. Get up, get out, and get in the booth, and vote for that person who has demonstrated that he has our best interest at heart. Amen!

THE CHURCH CONFRONTING THE CRISES OF THE EIGHTIES

(Matthew 16:18; Acts 2:41-47; Colossians 1:18)

The Word of the Lord: The logical and immediate question is what crises? We, as a people of Color, have known crises since setting foot on these shores centuries ago. We have been reared in the crucibles of crises. But we have always placed our hope, in times of crises, in the Creator and Sustainer of the universe. What are some elements of the crises that are prevalent today? Employment, education, housing, civil and human rights, political, social, and many others all have produced crises for us. In each of these categories, crises abound with which the Church must deal. Can and will the Church survive as she confronts the crises of the eighties? If we believe God's Word, and believe it to be infallible in all of its application, then we must say with resounding certainty: Yes, the Church will confront the crises and survive. Why are you so sure, you may ask?

Well, don't you remember the pronouncement that Christ made at the coast of Caesarea Philippi, as he anchored the faith of His disciples? He said to Peter, "…That thou art Peter, and upon this Rock I will build <u>MY</u> Church; and the <u>GATES</u> of hell shall not prevail against it." **(Matthew 16:18)** May I refresh your memory with respect to that immediate Post-Pentecostal Church? Dr. Luke gives us an insight in the second chapter of the Acts of the Apostles.

After Peter's sermon, as to whom Christ really was, they that gladly received his word were baptized and the same day, 3,000 souls were added to them. Do you recall that those new Pentecostals continued in the preacher's doctrine; they enjoyed wholesome fellowship, they broke and shared bread together, and ceased not to pray? They even went from house to house, breaking bread and edifying each other. They continued to praise the Lord, and received the favor of all the people, and as a consequence of this faithfulness; the Lord added to the Church daily, those that were being saved.

When we consider Paul's seven superiorities of Christ, as he lists them in his epistle to the Colossian believers, we can better understand why the Church will survive the crises of the eighties, and those beyond. Paul begins by declaring that "Christ is the image of the invisible God, the first born of every creature; For by him were all things created, that are in heaven, and that are in earth, visible and invisible, whether they be thrones, or dominions, or principalities, or powers: all things were created by him, and for him. And he is before all things, and by him, all things consist. And he is the head of the Body, the Church: who is the beginning, the first born from the dead; that in all things he might have the pre-eminence. For it pleased the Father that in Him should all fullness dwell" **(Colossians 1:15-19)**

We come this evening to present our case with respect to "Confronting the Crises of the Eighties." We come aware of the circumstances, conditions and times in which we live. We live in an age that is full of paradoxes, contrasts and conflicts. The sun of human knowledge is brightest since the rise of civilization and the dawn of history. By the testimony of philosophy and the deduction of science and the dreams and visions of our most gifted thinkers, man is nearer the peak of his mental potential today than any age of history. Man lives in an era when old, trusted foundations are shaking like leaves in the wind, and we are confronted with the severe test as to whether God still lives. Many men are debating whether the Church will decline and eventually become a mere social organization. The Church is unique because it is the oldest institution in the world today. Many kingdoms have risen and fallen; yet, the Church marches on stronger now than ever.

May we never forget that the sole source of the Church's life is Christ. We, the believers, are called the branches of the true vine, the body of Christ, the bride of the Church. The Bible is the only norm for an interpretation of the Church. It is a portrayal of the divine ideal, the divine principle, the divine purpose and the divine dynamic for the life of the Church. The Church is a spiritual fellowship, a living organism. It has life and the capacity to grow from within and without. It is made up of living stones that are held together by the Holy Spirit. The Church is the only ship that can navigate the stream of salvation. The river rises in creation, flows through time, empties into eternity, opened up by Jesus Christ, controlled by Jehovah God, and kept clean by the Holy Spirit.

The Church is unique because its Founder is unique. Jesus said, "…and upon this rock I will build My Church and the gates of hell shall not prevail against it." (**Matthew 16:18**) I will build MY CHURCH! It has been foretold by Zechariah that Christ should be the builder. He had said that the Messiah should build the Temple of the Lord and bear its glory. Here, Christ claims the prophecy as having spoken of Him and said, "I will build MY CHURCH."

I said the Founder is unique, for God has exalted Him so high until every knee shall bow and every tongue shall confess that He is King of Kings and Lord of Lords. His greatness is fully orbited. He was complete and in His completeness we find an explanation for His beauty. Men who stood nearest to Him were charmed and swayed by His loveliness. He was full of grace and truth. He had a charm about Him which wooed and fascinated men; children loved Him; boys sang for Him; publicans gathered around Him; and the multitudes followed Him; the blind found Him; the lame had hope in Him; and the world waited for Him.

Christ, the Head of the Church, was unique, because there has never been and never shall be another like Him. He was man and yet He was God. He put on humanity that we might put on divinity. He became the Son of man that we might become the sons of God. He came down from heaven where rivers never freeze, winds never blow, frost never chills the air, flowers never fade, sickness and death never come, and was born contrary to the laws of nature. Christ, the Head of the Church, was unique because He had no beginning and will have no ending. He lived and died, yet, He still lives! Men have opposed Him and plotted against Him and finally crucified Him on the cross of Calvary, but I heard Him speak to John on the Isle of Patmos one day and said, "I am He that liveth, and was dead; and behold, I am alive for evermore..." **(Revelation 1:18)**

May I hasten on now and say to you that the Church has had a unique history. It has its beginning in a cruel world where men had little or no regard for the will of God and the souls of men. The world, with all of its powers, came up against the Church. History reveals that the Church started out with a small band of men... twelve commonplace men; fishermen and tax collectors; men with meager education and training; but, He was determined to build His Church. History will reveal that the Church was persecuted, stoned and murdered, but this only gave rise to its growth.

Well, what will the end be? Certain institutional foundations are being shaken. What about the Church? Can and will it survive? Well, the Church is still influential today. Its influence has determined national developments, controlled social progress, fought against paganism and has guaranteed salvation for all men. It was nailed to the cross, but it shook that imperial throne to its death. Since Christ has entered humanity, a new power has been at work, a new force acquiring fresh momentum every year, and has been molding human affairs.

May I present one or two witnesses: Nicodemus, come here and give your story. Well, I was a Pharisee and a ruler of the Jews. I came to Jesus one night. **(John 3:1-12)** Come here Zacchaeus; tell your story. **(Luke 19:1-10)** Brother Paul, tell us your story. **(Acts 9:1-20)**

My friends, the Church will survive! Before Christ uttered His epochal words, as He journeyed to Jerusalem for His last visit, a solid foundation had been laid for the indestructibility of the Church. In getting the Church ready for its role, God looked through the telescope of time and selected a prophet by the name of Isaiah and had him to pen these words to Israel. Isaiah stated, "... And when you spread forth your hands, I will hide mine eyes from you: yea, when ye make many prayers, I will not hear: your hands are full of blood. Wash you, make you clean; put away the evil of your doings from before mine eyes; cease to do evil; Learn to do well; seek judgment, relieve the oppressed, judge the fatherless, plead for the widow. Come now, and let us reason together, saith the LORD: though your sins be as scarlet, they shall be as white as snow; though they be red like crimson, they shall be as wool. If ye be willing and obedient, ye shall eat the good of the land: But if ye refuse and rebel, ye shall be devoured with the sword: for the mouth of the LORD hath spoken it." **(Isaiah 1:15-20)**

Come here, Micah, what have you to say? The prophet posed this question: "Will the LORD be pleased with thousands of rams, or with ten thousands of rivers of oil? shall I give my first born for my transgression, the fruit of my body for the sin of my soul? He hath shewed thee, O man, what is good; and what doth the LORD require of thee, but to do <u>justly</u>, and to <u>love mercy</u>, and to <u>walk humbly</u> with thy God?" **(Micah 6:7-8)** Amos, come here. What is your contribution to this divine setting? Here's my answer: "... Let judgment run down as waters, and righteousness as a mighty stream." **(Amos 5:24)**

I hear the Lord say, "If I shut up heaven that there be no rain, or if I command the locusts to devour the land, or if I send pestilence among my people; If my people, which are called by my name, shall humble themselves, and pray, and seek my face, and turn from their wicked ways; then will I hear from heaven, and will forgive their sin, and will heal their land." **(2 Chronicles 7:13-14)**

"When Jesus came into the coasts of Caesarea Philippi, he asked His disciples, saying, Whom do men say that I the Son of man am? And they said, Some say that thou art John the Baptist; some, Elias; and others, Jeremias, or one of the prophets. He said unto them, But whom say ye that I am? And Simon Peter answered and said, Thou art the Christ, the Son of the living God. And Jesus answered and said unto him, Blessed art thou, Simon Bar-Jona: for flesh and blood hath not revealed it unto thee, but my Father which is in heaven. And I also say, also unto thee,

That thou art Peter, and upon this rock I will build my church; and the gates of hell shall not prevail against it." **(Matthew 16:13-18)**

"…All power is given unto me in heaven and in earth. Go ye therefore, and teach all nations, baptizing them in the name of the Father, and of the Son, and of the Holy Ghost: Teaching them to observe all things whatsoever I have commanded you: and, lo, I am with you always, even unto the end of the world. Amen." **(Matthew 28:18-20)**

"…And, behold, I send the promise of my Father upon you: but tarry ye in the city of Jerusalem, until ye be endued with power from on high." **(Luke 24:49)**

"…And the Lord added to the Church daily such as should be saved." **(Acts 2:47)**

Chapter Five

MY LOVELY WIFE, FLORA

✝

"Strength and honor are her clothing; and she rejoices in time to come," "Favour is deceitful, and beauty is vain, but a women who feareth the Lord, she shall be praised." **(Proverb 31:25, 30)**

Let me pause here, and speak about my lovely wife, Flora. This beautiful lady was a member of Emanuel since 1975. She was born in the state of Mississippi, the home of hospitality. Her father, the late Dennis Covington and mother, the late Jennie E. Covington, were strong Christian believers. Believe me when I say they were a close-knit family of twelve; six boys and six girls.

Upon her arrival in New York, I assisted her in finding employment. Her first employment was with the National Bank of North America, presently known as Bank of America. She was nurtured at the Emanuel Baptist Church as she grew spiritually and intellectually.

Her job at Bank of America enabled her to continue her education at New York University, from which she graduated in 1979 with a master of arts degree in office management and administration. She taught for many years in the private school sector in the areas of computer technology, stenography and administrative procedures.

When the secretary of Emanuel relocated to North Caroline, I asked Ms. Flora Covington to become the administrative assistant/office manager for Emanuel. She had a great personality and served well. She assisted contractors and the general manager in the construction of the New Emanuel Baptist Church. With all the responsibilities at the church, she opened and managed a small business know as **Parker and Parker Associates**, specializing in resume writing, research papers, doctoral reports and proposals. Every assignment given to her was done professionally and on time.

Her creativity and organizational skills were reflected in her daily work. In later years, she became president of the Board of Christian Education, Sunday school teacher for the young adults, and editor of the church monthly publication, *The Lighthouse*, which circulated in many parts of the United States and in foreign countries. She was a member of the Sunday school, Bible class, and Association for Female Executives, Top Ladies of Distinction and the Delta Sigma Theta sorority. As the years passed, she continued to grow spiritually at Emanuel.

I was a widower in 1987 with my ministry in high gear, as they say. I had completed my tenure as moderator of the Eastern Baptist

Association and was in the final stage of the construction of the New Emanuel. I shared a lot with my friends, Rich and Chuck, but it was nothing compared to going home and sharing personal thoughts with a mate. Yes, there were many women who were calling and asking; some tried to match me up with certain ones. I did not see the right one, or the Lord did not show me the right one. Maybe I was not ready for a helpmate. Anyhow, it was two years and I was still wandering around, preaching at every opportunity and traveling to various places. I was doing almost twenty-seven revivals a year. Then, the Spirit said, you need a helpmeet.

Well, after two years; yes, after two years, Flora and I started having dinner after Sunday morning worship service. It was wonderful to have someone to share with; a spiritual person who could understand my thoughts and offer suggestions. After about two months, one of my deacons came and said, "People are beginning to talk. You do not want to jeopardize your reputation." You know what happens when the stuff hit the fan. Church folk.

One Friday evening, I asked Flora, "Will you marry me?" and she looked as if I asked her to sky dive. Finally, she said, "I'll let you know." I knew what she had to do; she had to travel to Mississippi to talk to her mother and ALL of her sisters and brothers. I must say there was a LITTLE age difference of about thirty years, but we had a special and unique relationship. I knew that she was the one I wanted to spend the rest of my life with. After she returned from Mississippi, she said yes. I hurried out and bought a ring and after service that Sunday morning, I made the announcement. Well, without me writing another chapter, you can imagine how it went. I was wise enough to make this announcement at the close of the service. The telephone lines were busy for hours; the news had travelled from New York to yonder. My favorite song was, **"I Am Happy With Jesus Alone."** One of the members met me at the back door and said, "I thought you said that you were happy with Jesus alone." Flora was as cool and charming as ever. Some members congratulated us and some were in disbelief. Either way, we went out to eat that afternoon and started making plans for the wedding.

The wedding was on Saturday, August 12, 1989. There was a thunderstorm; it rained most of the day. We claimed it as showers of blessings from above. The groomsmen were in place looking spiffy; the bridesmaids were in place looking glamorous. The minister came out of the office to perform the wedding. I was so nervous that I turned to look as if I were officiating. I was told to turn around, that I was not in charge. To see my new bride walk down the aisle was a gift from heaven; a temporary memory lapse on my part. Her brother William, from Flint, Michigan, gave her away. After the reception he said, "I am giving her to you, don't let me have to come back up here." I must say here that he never had to come back. We were in the Lord's hand; it was all part of God's divine will for my life.

We planned our honeymoon in Paris, France. We left New York early Monday morning on our way to Paris. We had hotel reservation at the Concorde Lafayette, in the heart of the city, twenty-fourth floor. I remember when the taxi driver learned of the hotel in which we were to stay, he wanted to know if we wanted a cheaper hotel. Our answer was definitely "no." We could look out of our window and see the Eiffel Towel. I had been stationed in France while in the military, and was able to speak the language, not fluently, but well. While other visitors were paying $60 for the tour bus, Flo and I got a map from the tour desk and we travelled by subway. When they arrived at the location, we were already there. We spent two-and-a-half weeks in Paris and had the opportunity to visit many historical places, which included a cruise down the Seine River.

It was now time to return to my duties as pastor of Emanuel, and with a new bride walking beside me. What a challenge!!

Flora had been a member of Emanuel for approximately twelve years and knew somewhat of the relationship of being the wife of a pastor. However, to better understand her role, she joined the Ministers' Wives and Widows Fellowship of the Eastern Baptist Association, where there was a group of seasoned ministers' wives who were willing and able to lead and guide her in the right direction. Some had been the wife of a pastor for some thirty years. I knew she was in good hands, because the past president, Marie Moses, was in my cabinet, and the president at the present time, Marva Corley, and others were most gracious and kind to her. I must say that she learned beyond her years because I believe she was the youngest member of the ministers' wives group. After many years of participation with the ladies, she became dean of the group and an area vice president of Nassau County. I was so proud of her. She was a Christian woman, had great organizational skills, spoke well, and was able to adjust to the life of a pastor's wife, the church family, and my chaotic schedule. I did not ask her to accompany me to every place that I went because this was all new to her and I knew she had to grow in the ministry. As I said, I had been around for a while. However, she wanted to accompany me to many of my engagements. The good wife, not the one who plays the role on television, but the one the Lord sent just for me. I can say with confidence, that with my pastoral experience and her encouragement and motivation, we were comfortable working as a team. The Lord continued to bless us as we walked and worked together.

Every year in August was my vacation month; Flo and I planned a trip to Hawaii. We visited four of the islands including the Big Island. One day we decided to rent a car in Maui and drive to the top of the mountain. Some of the tourists were driving to the top to witness the sunrise; we had no such intentions. However, we started up the mountain with no side railings and only one way up. We drove ten thousand feet above the clouds (we have pictures standing above the clouds) and when we parked, the air was light and we were told to walk slowly because of the altitude. I can tell you now, if we had to do it again, it would never happen. Flo was right beside me, scared to look out the window because I was driving. And just to let you know, there was nothing really exciting up there to see.

When we made it back to the foot of the mountain (earth), we said, "Thank You, Lord; that will not happen again."

The next year's vacation we decided to do something different; something a little less dramatic. We planned a pilgrimage to Africa, Dakar Senegal. Eighteen members from Emanuel and from various churches travelled with us. Now this was a cultural experience. We were told by the travel agent to carry with us fifty single dollar bills; no explanation. When we got to the hotel, a hundred or more children were there begging for money. Before we knew it, our fifty dollars were all gone. However, we were happy to be able to share. We took daily trips: the Gold Coast, the Door of No Return, and had a chance to speak with the village chiefs. We saw a need there. One of the cultural shocks was to see lepers in the city. These were people with leprosy (a half body and half dysfunctional), something that we never read about; not in the history book. For many months after the trip, we had constant thoughts of this knowledge after returning back to New York. From that moment, we decided we had nothing of which to complain, only hearts of thanksgiving. We promised ourselves not to be wasteful, to make sacrifices, and to always give as the Spirit leads. We kept in contact with the village chiefs and sent supplies, clothes and other materials from the Emanuel Baptist Church that were requested. All of this inspired me to give continually to the National Baptist Foreign Mission. Flo was a real trooper; an excellent organizer. I loved her more each day. She stayed on top of things and I was able to focus more on my ministry while she planned and advised in other areas.

I have to stop here and give the highest thanks for my lovely wife, because as I mentioned earlier, she was a graduate with a master's degree in management and could have had a full-time job with a six-figure salary, but the Lord joined us together to fulfill His divine will. She worked at places where she was able to travel with me and was also able to explain to her supervisors and directors that her life was with her husband. With her many sacrifices, I promised that I would take excellent care of her for as long as the Lord granted this union. With her support and cheerfulness, the church grew spiritually and financially. Flora made sure that I had the best. When I reached seventy years of age, she organized a birthday celebration, surprise, surprise! The same thing happened again at seventy-five, eighty, eighty-five and then ninety. I really thought that I could not be surprised, but Flora always pulled it off. She was an amazing woman!

We started attending conventions together. Namely, the Empire Baptist Missionary Convention, where I later served as area vice president for The Long Island Shore area, and she became an active part of the Ministers' Wives and Widows Auxiliary. In the latter years of faithful and dedicated service, she wore the title, **"Centennial Queen"** of the Empire Baptist Convention, Ministers' Wives and Widows Auxiliary, a title that can only be granted once. She accompanied me to the National Baptist Convention, where I became Representative of the United Nation for the Convention and, yes, she was appointed as my UN Assistant. I heard one say "team-work makes the dream work." We were the "A" team.

On our own, and with the support of Emanuel, we travelled to others countries to gather information that would be pertinent to the convention. This is another story, in another chapter. However, at the request of one of Emanuel's trustees, we were invited to provide service in St. Vincent, the West Indies. It was the work of the Lord. We completed a week of revival. Souls were saved, we give God the glory. The scary part of the trip was flying to our place of abode. Only four of us were able to fit on the plane (a small chopper), and it landed in the fields on a dirt path. Flo and I looked at each other and at that point determined that we were not going to get back on that small plane. At the close of the week, we were driven back to the airport by the pastor; it took three-and-a-half hours of travel time. It was perfectly okay with us.

Flora enjoyed church work. She continued to be a faithful member of the Bible class each Saturday; a member of the Adult Choir and also continued teaching the young adult Sunday school class. She had a keen interest in the youth, using her talents and skills to aid them in career development, personality development, and self-esteem. She set up a mentoring program (Big Sisters) to help the youth in the church and community to develop their fullest potential. She assisted with Vacation Bible School each year, and was the Women Day speaker at various churches in the Metropolitan area and as far as Washington, DC. She spoke at one church in Long Island, New York for four consecutive years. I was about to put a lid on it, however, Flora never tried to overshadow me. She found where she could use her skills most and continued to enhance my ministry.

To show our appreciation, each year, she was honored with a "First Lady's Appreciation Service." Everything was done in the Spirit of love. And of course, I always presented her with a dozen roses for her exemplary leadership and stickability. Well done, Flo!!

Now, it is August again, and we are planning another vacation. This year we planned a trip to Jerusalem, accompanied by eighteen members of Emanuel and others from area churches. Each trip was a learning experience. We (Flo and I) never thought we would have the opportunity to walk where Jesus walked; to walk through the Garden of Gethsemane; dip our feet in the Dead Sea; go up by cable car to Masada; and to be able to preach on Peter's boat (the sea of Galilee). Flora said Amen, as I spoke in the Upper Room. Only God knew His plan for us when He joined us together. After our many cultural experiences, and as I was moving up in age, we made plans to travel to Ocean City, Maryland; a place of quiet and relaxation. Yes, Flora drove each year without complaint.

And so now, it comes time for my retirement. Flora said, "That is between you and the Lord. When you are ready, I am ready."

We made plans to move to Baltimore, Maryland. We made trips to and from New York to make sure things were going smoothly.

You can almost guess who did all the packing and organizing. The Lord showed us the land; the right location.

This year, 2008, we are celebrating her nineteenth appreciation service. I penned these words to her to express my love and appreciation for her many years of love and dedication. And the Lord gave us twenty-five years together.

To my dearest helpmeet, Flora D.

*It is with resounding pleasure and satisfaction that I extend to you my most sincere congratulations and best wishes as you observe your well-deserved 19th **First Lady's Appreciation Service**. I am proud of you and I wish you much happiness on this occasion that honors you for your steadfastness as the "**First Lady of The Emanuel Baptist Church**." I know from experience that it is not easy being the wife and confidant of a pastor; nevertheless, you have proven, without a doubt, your worthiness and dedication to the position as the "Leading Lady."*

You are my anchor and my loving companion who works tirelessly to encourage me as I perform my numerous tasks as pastor. Your input is reflected in every aspect of my life. For instance: when I view my office at home; the neat arrangement of my office files; the progress that I have made in the area of modern technology. I must give you credit for any proficiency that I have achieved. Yes, Flora D., I can see the imprints of your hand in my ministries. And regardless of the task, you are always present to assist me. For this, I thank you!

*As I pen this brief note, I must pause to give thanks to my Heavenly Father for sending you to walk with me through this life. When my Father looked at my life, He determined that I needed a helpmeet to stand by and with me. My Heavenly Father knew a "**PASTOR**" needed a special person; a person who could provide a stable and pleasant atmosphere in the home; who could communicate with all people and who could represent me at functions and encompass my desires. Yes, again, I thank my Heavenly Father for sending you to me; you, who understands the "**real me**." And so as I look back over these past nineteen years, I must say that much of my success can be attributed to your unconditional love, support, cooperation, and understanding. I know that without you standing by me and with me, my secular life would have been all but empty! Enjoy this occasion, "Flora." I love you now, tomorrow and forever!*

Forever Yours, "H.D."

Shortly after the nineteenth anniversary, we relocated to Baltimore, Maryland. On August 12, 2014, the Lord gave us twenty-five blissful years together. He is worthy to be praised!

"Who can find a virtuous woman? For her price is above rubies." (**Proverbs 31:10**)

Chapter Six

THE EMPIRE BAPTIST MISSIONARY CONVENTION OF NEW YORK

I n October, 1965, the Empire Baptist Missionary Convention of New York met at the Bethany Baptist Church, in Syracuse, New York. The honored president is the Reverend Dr. Sandy F. Ray. Two years after my call to the pastorate of the Emanuel Baptist Church, I was asked to respond to the welcome. A surprise it was; however, I am always ready for a challenge.

I must preface my remarks by assuring you that I feel highly honored having been asked to respond to the welcome address on this auspicious occasion. With a keen sense of humility, I accept this cherished honor with profound gratitude.

The splendid welcome we have received portrays the high regard in which our convention is held, and I am extremely happy, as I know you are, to be a member of such a renowned organization.

I know, too, that I echo the sentiments of this august body when I say that the welcome address, so eloquently delivered by the distinguished pastor who preceded me, the Reverend Dr. Leo Murphy, has electrified us, by dispelling all doubt that might have plagued our minds. It has crystalized our assurance that we are welcomed here with open arms. The hospitality shown by our hosts and the people of this city overwhelms me, and I stand tonight to tell you of the appreciation of the guests for the welcome you have given us.

I feel that I could talk for hours about this fine city and the friendly people who live here. The hospitality for its visitors, which has always been characteristic of this city, has not diminished through the years. It is a unique privilege for us to be its guests.

I am persuaded to employ here the language of the spokesman of that select group, who met in executive session with Christ on the Mt. of Transfiguration, and cried with resplendent joy, "Lord, it is good for us to be here!" It is with this spirit of gratitude that we accept the expressions of greetings from the hearts and lips of this community. We are grateful to know that you have opened to us the doors of your homes, your hotels, your motels, and other essential facilities. We assure you that your facilities and your generosity will not be abused.

I came prepared to deliver a somewhat lengthy response, knowing that this was an excellent opportunity to say something complimentary about the fine people who make up this great convention. I spent considerable time in search of proper words of praise for members of this convention, and now I discover that I am in somewhat the same position as the man whose mule became sick. The man went to a veterinarian to get some medicine for the animal. The doctor prescribed the medicine and advised him to place it in a tube and blow it down the mule's throat. While trying to follow these simple instructions, however, the man met with disaster. He ran to the veterinarian, nursing a bit of discomfort, and cried out, *"Doctor, the mule blowed first!"* In the same way, I was going to blow about this fine convention, but the distinguished speaker who offered such a cordial welcome, *"Done blowed first!"*

But seriously, ladies and gentlemen, we are here, not on a pleasure trip, but to be about "our Father's business." We are here to make a wise investment of our time, our talents, and our tithes in the world-wide enterprise of advancing God's Kingdom. When we think of the challenge that confronts this annual session, who has adopted the provocative theme: "FREEDOM WITH JUSTICE AND RESPONSIBILITY," and when we consider our purpose in being here, we must turn back the pages of history to recapture the purpose for which Christ came into the world nearly 2,000 years ago.

Why did He come? The sacred records record the answers: He came to seek and to save that which was lost. He came as the God-sent, the heavenly legate, with the instrument of peace written by the finger of the Father's hand. He came to bind up the broken-hearted, and to cheer the millions with the message of love. He came to give sight to the blind and strength to the weak. He came to Nain to give life to the widow's son and joy to a mother's heart. He came to Gadara, where the legion of devils fled at His command and plunged headlong into the raging sea. The angry storm on the frosty bosom of the Sea of Galilee heard His invincible voice and the waters ceased to dance to the music of the winds. At Jericho, blind Bartimaeus saw the bright light of heaven by the healing power of the Master's touch.

At Bethesda, He fed 5,000 with a little lad's lunch. He raised Lazarus from his four-day grave slumber, and told that awe-struck crowd to "Loose the man and let him Go!" He expelled the palsy, scattered fevers, dried up issues of blood, and restored the withered hand. That is why He came. And this is why we come. We come because He said Go! In His Great Commission message, He uttered these solemn words: "Go ye therefore and teach all Nations...."

Yes, this is why we have come. We do not seek an easy task; we simply ask for grace and strength. Finally, we have come to perpetuate the work begun by this great convention seventy years ago. The task will not be easy. But we are proud of our heritage. We are also proud of our president, Dr. Sandy F. Ray, who has been at the helm of this ship, guiding her destiny, for the past ten years.

Our president will demonstrate during this session, as he has at all previous sessions of his administration, that he is the man of the hour; the man to whom we may look with justifiable pride for his ability, courage, forthright leadership, and determination;

the man who will continue to lead the Empire Baptist Missionary Convention to higher heights, and to achieve goals which at first might seem impossible. But, we have a great leader in Dr. Ray. Someone has stated so aptly that a leader is anyone who is endowed with two characteristics: First, he is going somewhere; and secondly, he is able to persuade others to go with him.

The success of this great convention depends not only upon the conscientious work of our devoted president, but upon every messenger in attendance here. "Only a genius can achieve without labor and more often than not, the achievement is an accident. But one who prepares for achievement by a keen study of the situation, by acquiring knowledge of his possibilities and purposes, by knowing the elements necessary to its proper understanding and the rules and methods of applying them, is certain to attain success."

And so, my friends, on behalf of our beloved president, the official family of our Great Empire Baptist Missionary Convention, and the messengers assembled here from throughout this great Empire State, once again, we accept your kind welcome with humility and profound gratitude.

It was an honor to be asked to respond to the welcome for the Empire Baptist Convention. As stated earlier, I was a new pastor of only two years; I was not a regular attendee of the state convention. My main focus was establishing a strong relationship with Emanuel. I spent most of my time working, planning and organizing events for spiritual growth. However, in later years, I did start attending, regularly, the semi and annual sessions. Many of my members became state officers.

I had the privilege of serving with five state presidents: Reverend Eckols, Reverend Sam Austin, Reverend Allen A. Stanley, Reverend Robert W. Dixon and Reverend Washington L. Lundy.

In 1991, I was elected area vice president of the Empire Baptist Missionary Convention, serving the Long Island Shore Area, consisting of Nassau and Suffolk Counties. It was a pleasant experience because most of the brethren were close associates. I had the privilege of speaking at numerous banquets, pastors' anniversaries, and kept pastors abreast of programs and events pertinent to the convention. My duties were what I loved most, speaking with ministers to encourage growth and stability in ministry, and in the church.

After my tenure as area vice president, I was appointed a member of the advisory committee and member of the Constitution and By-Laws Committee. I give God my best in all things.

After many years of dedicated and faithful service, in 2002, I was asked to give the closing sermon at the semi-annual session. What a mighty God we serve.

LOOKING AT THE CHURCH THROUGH THE EYES OF JESUS

(Matthew 9:36-38)

This is Empire; and Empire will continue to move onward and upward under the leadership of our serious and determined president, Robert W. Dixon.

The Word of God. I have been given the theme from which to speak at this *Semi-Annual Session,* May 9, 2002. However, I have chosen a supplemental theme, and I beg your indulgence to accept it: **"The Compassionate Christ."** The Scriptures reads, "But when he saw the multitudes, he was moved with compassion on them, because they fainted, and were scattered abroad, as sheep having no shepherd. Then saith he unto his disciples, The harvest truly is plenteous, but the labourers are few; Pray ye therefore the Lord of the harvest, that he will send forth labourers into HIS harvest." (**Matthew 9:36-38**). We consider, now, those same verses from the Good News Bible in Today's English Version. "As he saw the crowds, his heart was filled with pity for them, because they were worried and helpless, like sheep without a shepherd. So He said to His disciples, 'The harvest is large, but there are few workers to gather it in. Pray to the owner of the harvest that he will send out workers to gather in the harvest.'"

As I looked at this theme and the references from which it was derived, it became necessary for me to dissect, analyze, explain and reconstruct, because we as finite beings find it impossible to see through the infinite eyes of Jesus, the Christ. Finite though we may be, I believe that it is possible for us, somehow, to surmise His interest and focus by considering the nature of His divine attributes since He is divine in its fullness. Therefore, looking at the church through His infinite eyes, we are able to behold the church through the eyes of the **Omnipotent** Christ who has infinite power. It was through those eyes, those omnipotent eyes that our Christ gazed upon a restless and tempestuous sea as he "…rebuked the wind, and said unto the sea, Peace, be still." The record is "the wind ceased, and there was a great calm" (**Mark 4:39**).

It was through those **Omnipotent** eyes, tempered with loving compassion, that He looked out upon the mournful congregation of family and friends at the graveside of Lazarus. After declaring Himself to be the resurrection and the life, He wept. After lifting up those all-seeing eyes toward heaven, He prayed. Following His brief instructions to roll away the stone from the grave's entrance, the record is, "…and when he had thus spoken, he cried with a loud voice, Lazarus, come forth. And he that was dead came forth, bound hand and foot with grave clothes: and his face was bound about with a napkin. Jesus saith unto them, Loose him, and let him go." (**John 11:43-44**)

It can be biblically verified that many other acts of healing, raising the dead, multiplying scarce food supplies, as well as His pre-incarnate work in the creation and maintaining the world, all attest to His infinite power as cataloged in the divine records. For example, in Paul's epistle to the Colossian believers, the apostle makes this assertion, "In whom we have redemption through his blood, even the forgiveness of sins: Who is the image of the invisible God, the firstborn of every creature: For by him were all things created, that are in heaven and that are in earth, visible and invisible whether they be thrones, or dominion, or principalities, or power: all things were created by Him, and for Him: And He is before all things, and by him all things consists." (**Colossians 1:14-17**)

Looking at the church through the eyes of Jesus, one must also look through **Omnipresent** eyes; meaning that He is everywhere, present in space and time at the same time. Therefore, looking through His eyes, we are looking through the eyes of Him who declared, "Your father Abraham rejoiced to see my day: and he saw it, and was glad. ...Verily, verily, I say unto you, Before Abraham was, I am." (**John 8:56-58**)

We observe His omnipresent posture in the calling of Nathaniel. I hear Him say in **John 1:48**, "Nathaniel saith unto him, Whence knowest thou me? Jesus answered and said unto him, Before Philip that called thee, when thou wast under the fig tree, I saw thee." Yes, we see His **Omnipresent** posture expressed in His Great Commission to His disciples at the end of His earthly mission. Do you hear Him speak to them, after His resurrection and prior to His ascension back to His Father? *What did He say?* "Go ye therefore, and teach all nations, baptizing them in the name of the Father, and of the Son, and of the Holy Ghost: Teaching them to observe all things whatsoever I have commended you; and lo, I am with you always, even unto the end of the world. Amen." (**Matthew 28:19-20**)

It is to be noted here that the writers of Proverbs, said to be Solomon and others, had this to say on the subject: "The eyes of the Lord are in every place, beholding the evil and the good." (**Proverbs 15:3**) <u>**Omnipresence**</u>, if you will!

Looking at the church through the eyes of Jesus demands that we look at the church through the eyes of one who is **Omnicient** or all-knowing in nature. He, therefore, is not baffled by what He observes because of His infinite and complete knowledge of all things. John gives credence and verification to this fact in the record of the gospel that bears his name. John records, "Now when he was in Jerusalem at the Passover in the feast day, many believed in his name, when they saw the miracles which he did. But Jesus did not commit himself unto them, because he knew all men, and needed not that any should testify of man: for he knew what was in man." (**John 2:23-25**) Throughout the gospels, the writers state this fact, "Jesus knew their hearts." "Jesus perceived their thoughts." "He knew all about man."

I must also state that looking at the church through the eyes of Jesus demands that we look at the church through **loving** and **compassionate** eyes. Sadly though, this is not always the case. As revealed in our text and interwoven throughout the gospel record, the Spirit of these words is recorded: "But when he saw the multitude he moved with compassion on them, because they fainted and were scattered abroad as sheep having no shepherd." **Matthew 9:36,** our text, states that when He saw the multitude He was moved with compassion on them because they fainted and were scattered abroad as sheep having no shepherd. It should be pointed out at this juncture that there were other times that His look brought about different responses. For example, each of the gospel writers records where He, upon entering the temple and observing the activities going on there, He became, as theologians choose to state, "filled with righteous indignation." In other words, He became angry and overthrew the table of the money changers and the seats of them that sold doves and would not suffer any man to carry any vessel through the temple. He said on that occasion, "It is written, My house is the house of prayer: but ye have made it a den of thieves." **(Luke 19:46)**

Yes, but this day, as seen in our text, when He see them, He is moved with compassion on them. Compassion, as defined by Webster, is a feeling of deep sympathy and sorrow for another's suffering or misfortune, accompanied by a desire to alleviate the pain or remove its cause. My sisters and my brothers, it is this feeling of compassion that has become the most identifying characteristic of our Lord. As seen throughout the scripture, acts of physical healing have always been motivated by divine compassion. Jeremiah tells us, "It is of the Lord's mercies that we are not consumed, because his compassions fail not." (**Lamentation 3:22**)

Needless to say, as we look at the church through His eyes, who can ignore His many acts of physical healing as recorded in the gospel? To mention just a few: The two blind men who made their way through a crucial and critical crowd which stood to oppose them as they cried out in unison, "Have mercy on us, O Lord, thou Son of David. And Jesus stood still and called them, and said, What will ye that I shall do unto you? They said unto him, 'Lord, that our eyes may be opened.' So Jesus had compassion on them, and touched their eyes: and immediately their eyes received sight, and they followed him." (**Matthew 20:30-34**) Mark tells us of a leper who came to Jesus, who kneeled down to Him and uttered these solemn words, "If thou wilt, thou canst make me clean. And Jesus, moved with compassion, and saith unto him, 'I will; be thou clean.' And as soon as he had spoken, immediately the leprosy departed from him, and he was cleansed." (**Mark 1:40-42**)

Yes, Jesus is a man of compassion. In Mark 9:22, we see Jesus at the foot of the mountain of transfiguration when the cry for compassion came by the father of the demon-possessed boy; Jesus responded and healed the lad. Jesus showed compassion toward the hungry multitude by feeding them on two different occasions. (**Mark 5:19**) Time does not permit me to enumerate all of the times that Jesus showed compassion upon those who came to Him.

In our text today, Jesus observed a greater need than mere physical. He observed that there was the need for spiritual rejuvenation. He saw them as sheep scattered across the hills and plains of lostness and needing to be found. He saw them as wounded sheep needing the anointing oil of healing grace. He saw them as hungry and spiritually destitute sheep needing, not only to be fed by a loving, caring shepherd, but He saw them needing to be fed with the bread of hope and comforted with the joy of salvation. He saw them!

He saw them from both the Old and the New Testaments' perspective. From the Old, He saw them as the lost sheep of the house of Israel; stumbling and mortally wounded by a broken law and going astray, and who would not gather them. He saw them from the New Testament perspective; He saw them in the midst of the wolves of a vicious society with no shepherd or the wrong shepherds, who did not provide the proper care and concern for them. In the case where there was no shepherd, He saw the awesome need that they had. In those cases where they had the wrong shepherds, He looked beyond their big degrees and impressive titles. He looked beyond their eloquent discourses and persuasive charismatic persona. He looked beyond their display of elegant attire and flashy possessions. With great compassion, He looked at them (the church) and saw them as scattered sheep wandering without a shepherd. He looks at those scattered sheep whose needs can be met only by those faithful shepherds obedient to the call of God, who for the love of Christ, obey His commandment to "Go ye therefore and teach all nations, baptizing them in the name of the Father and of the Son, and of the Holy Ghost: Teaching them to observe all things whatsoever that I have commanded you: and lo, I am with you always even unto the end of the world. Amen." (**Matthew 28:16-20**) Yes, the ready harvest is an obvious fact, but such laborers as they need must be sent by the Father into His harvest. Pray for such laborers in full commitment and the end results may be as the prophet of old states: "Here am I; Send me."

Look at the Man! Look at Jesus! The Bible declares that when He departed from there; i.e., His hometown Capernaum, two blind men followed Him, crying, and saying, "Thou Son of David, have mercy on us." Jesus asked them this simple question, "Believe ye that I am able to do this?" They said, "Yea, Lord." This Christ of compassion simply touched their eyes and they were opened. I hear Jesus say to them, "Don't tell anyone; See that no man knows it." The record is that a demon-possessed man was brought to Him, and He cast the demon out of him. The demon began to speak and the people marveled. We have not seen this in all Israel. And following the criticism of the Pharisees, Jesus went about all the cities and villages, teaching in their synagogues, and preaching the gospel of the kingdom, and healing every sickness and every disease among the people.

And now we see Him in our text, "...then saith he unto the disciples, "The harvest truly is great, but the labourers are few:

pray ye therefore the Lord of the harvest, that he would send forth labourers into his harvest." **(Luke 10:2)** Friends…you and I on whom Christ has placed this responsibility to go out into the highways and hedges, we have a mandate from Him to do just that. There is no time for indulging in petty rivalries. There are souls out there that need to hear the unfailing Gospel of Jesus Christ. The highways and the hedges, they are there. In your neighborhood, in my neighborhood, they are there waiting to hear the Gospel of Jesus Christ. What will you do?

If I were to call Isaiah to the stand, Isaiah would say, "It was in the year that King Uzziah died, I saw, also, the Lord sitting upon a throne, high and lifted up, and his train filled the temple." Isaiah would describe what he saw in the temple. And finally, Isaiah would say, "One of the seraphim took a live coal from the altar and laid it on my lips and confirmed to me that my iniquity had been taken away and my sin purged." Isaiah would tell us that after this incident with the Seraphim, he heard the voice of the Lord, saying, "Whom shall I send, and who will go for us? Then said I, Here am I; send me." **(Isaiah 6:8)**

I don't know about you, but I made Him a promise more than sixty-five years ago, that I would serve Him. I have been on the battlefield a long time; but, I am not tired yet. There is more work to be done. I am not tired yet. Why? There is a crown! There is a crown! There is a crown waiting for me in that New Jerusalem.

Chapter Seven

A RENOWNED RADIO PERSONALITY

I met Reverend H. David Parker, or "Pop" as I lovingly called him, in the spring of 1996. I had just become the afternoon drive personality at WTHE-AM in Mineola where "Pop" did his daily broadcast, "Morning Meditations." I had been working there about a month when he unexpectedly showed up at the radio station.

The station manager came into the control room and she looked somewhat worried. She was somewhat of the nervous type, so when I asked her what was wrong she said, "Reverend Parker is here." I have to admit, I was taken aback as to why she was so nervous. So I said, "Okay so, what does that have to do with me?" She informed me that he wanted to see me and if he made a special trip to the radio station to see me, it couldn't be good. WTHE was a gospel radio station that played primarily traditional gospel music. I came in, pretty much out of the blue, playing contemporary and hip hop gospel music along with the traditional music. Needless to say, this was not well received by some of the regular listeners. So, she was sure he was here to complain in person.

In typical Brooklyn, New York, fashion, I told her to tell him to have a seat and I'll come out after I change the record. Well, she looked at me like I had three heads at my response and then she said, "Nobody keeps Reverend Parker waiting; you need to come out right now!" So, I cut the song that was playing and put on a long version of "I Won't Complain" by Reverend Paul Jones, which is almost eleven minutes long, and came out to meet the person who caused this uproar.

When I got to the lobby, I saw a distinguished older gentleman, dressed in a black suit with a pastor's collar. His face showed the wisdom of the ages and although he was not a very large man, just average in size, he had a presence about him that made him seem bigger than life. Before I could say anything he said, "You must be Brother Darren Greggs," I said, "Yes sir, I am. You must be Reverend Parker." He responded, "The one and only." Then, we both shared the first of many laughs together. He then proceeded to explain the reason for his visit.

He told me, "I wanted to meet the man who was doing such a great job on the air." To this day, I'm not sure who was more relieved to hear his reason for the visit, me or the station manager. He then proceeded to encourage me to keep doing what I was doing regardless of the reaction of some of the listeners. He explained that the hardest thing to do is make people change. In that five-minute meeting, GOD used him to validate me and my life was never the same.

His radio program, "Morning Meditations," was more than just a radio show. "Morning Meditations," was an institution. For over thirty-three years, it seemed that all of Long Island, New York paused to hear what Reverend Parker had to say. Needless to say, "Pop" never disappointed. In fact, I often found myself reserving opinion concerning some hot button issues until I heard what Reverend Parker had to say on the subject.

About three months after this initial meeting, I was promoted to program director and I moved to the morning show. This allowed me to speak to "Pop" every morning because his program aired Monday through Friday at 8:15 am. Reverend Parker was probably the most disciplined man I ever met. He would either call or show up at the radio station at 8:10. Not 8:11 or 8:09, 8:10 exactly. Now that I think about it, in the over ten years that I engineered his program, he was late less than ten times. More often than not, he would call me the day before to tell me he was going to be late.

I once told him that I never met a person who was as punctual and disciplined as he was. He then, told me something that I will never forget. He told me, "Time is something that you can't save. Once time is gone, you can't get it back. So, you should never waste time. You should use it wisely."

I looked forward to the five minutes before "Pop" did his show, because that was when I got the opportunity to get the pearls of wisdom that fell from him. He would counsel me, laugh with me, cry with me and when necessary, correct me. He would tell me about his time in the military and his experiences as a pastor. He quickly became one of my dearest friends.

Reverend Parker, unselfishly, shared his wisdom with me and he grew into one of the greatest and most positive influences in my life. When I met him, I had separated from my wife and was going through a very long and bitter divorce. I had a son from that marriage and it was a very difficult time for me. I was often depressed, I felt like a failure and worst of all, I couldn't see my son like I wanted to.

GOD used Reverend Parker and those five minutes before his program to lift me out of depression and to show me that because my marriage failed, I wasn't a failure. Because of that I was able to reclaim my life, and most importantly, be a father to my son, regardless of the circumstances.

When Reverend Parker retired and moved to Maryland, there was a void, not only at WTHE but also in my life. I quickly missed my daily dose of wisdom and laughter. I even missed the organ music that played behind him as he did his show. Our daily conversations turned to once every couple of months. Then eventually just on holidays and birthdays.

When GOD called "Pop" home to his well-deserved reward, I felt lost for a moment. Then GOD reminded me of what I learned at the feet of Reverend Parker. I was also reminded of where I was when GOD brought "Pop" into my life; how he was used to bring me out of a cold, dark place to a place of light and warmth. I will never forget the words of wisdom he shared with me, the jokes we told, the cups of coffee we drank together and most importantly, the love we had for each other.

Today, when I think of him, as I often do, I always remember how he ended his program. He would play the song, "Have You Stopped To Pray This Morning," and say, "No day is well spent without a talk with the LORD."

Hey "Pop," see you in Glory…

Darren Greggs

Program Director

Radio Station: WTHE 1520, Mineola, New York

Chapter Eight

THE NATIONAL BAPTIST CONVENTION, USA, INC

After being installed as pastor of the Emanuel Baptist Church of Elmont, Long Island, New York, on February 17, 1963, the fifth pastor in the history of the church, I made a decision to attend the National Baptist Convention that was meeting in the state of Ohio. I left New York City by train on a Monday morning, having previously made reservations for both my train trip and hotel reservation in Ohio.

Having settled in my seat for the journey, an elderly gentleman came down the aisle and stopped at my seat. He asked me: "Young man, where are you going?" I responded by informing him that I was on my way to the convention in Ohio. "Is this your first time attending the convention?" I responded, "Yes; this is my first visit to the convention." He went on to ask me if I was married. I responded, "Yes, I am married." "Your wife is not with you; are you meeting someone there?" I thought the question was somewhat strange, and I did not know, then, what he was insinuating. Later years, the answer came to me. I guess I was a little slow, or as they say, green around the edge.

After many years of association with the National Baptist Convention, it became important to me to attend each annual session. I went as a pastor/leader of God's people representing the Emanuel Baptist Church. Each year, almost twenty years, approximately eight to ten delegates accompanied me to the convention. We attended workshops, seminars, preaching and teaching. We did not attend the convention to waste time, shopping, eating, greeting, but to improve ourselves in Christian education.

I had the privilege of being in the presence of six dynamic presidents: Dr. Joseph H. Jackson (J.H.), Dr. Theodore Judson Jemison (T.J.), Dr. S. E. Cureton, Dr. Henry J. Lyons, Dr. William J. Shaw, and Dr. Julius Scruggs. What an honor.

In 1995, I was appointed by Dr. Henry J. Lyons as the National Baptist Convention, USA, Representative to the United Nations. I served as the person responsible for monitoring and reporting on the activities and decisions of the United Nations relative to the international interests of the National Baptist Convention. After receiving my official certification in April 1995, I was given the opportunity to vote for the slate of officers for the Executive Committee on the NGO/DPI Division. I was asked to give my report to the convention at each annual session. Each Tuesday, I was present at the United Nations' General Assembly in New York City. My function has been basically to observe and to exercise my judgement as to what I felt would be of primary interest, national and international, to our convention. I was honored to be one of the 1,437 Non-Governmental Organizational Representatives, with more that forty countries involved as of June 8, 1995.

On my second visit to the United Nations, the Honorable Leona S. Foreman, Chief of the NGO/DPI (Non-Governmental Organization/ Department of Information Division) invited NGOs to submit ideas and suggestions to aid in strengthening and enhancing the operation of the department. I did what I knew best. I recommended that each session of our department open with prayer. In my previous visits, there was never any mention or recognition of a Supreme Being. In my judgement, if the United States was about global peace, I believed it was incumbent upon its representatives to recognize a Supreme Being as the only source of peace.

In August 1996, I made a trip to Dakar, Senegal, West Africa, where I spent ten days of what I termed, "**A Visit to the Mother Land**." While in Dakar, I paid an unofficial visit to the US Embassy, where I met informally with the vice consul, the Honorable Nathan V. Holt. I had been approached by several individuals in Dakar who desired a three-month visa to the United States. Ambassador Holt assured me that if a request was initiated on behalf of an individual whom I felt would enhance the relations between our convention and certain individuals from the Senegalese community, such request would receive favorable consideration. I, also, paid a courtesy visit to the office of the Honorable Abdoulaye Wade, who serves as secretary general of the Senegalese Democratic Party.

Accompanying me on this historical venture were twenty members from the Emanuel Baptist Church. It was our privilege to visit the infamous Goree Island, where millions of our foreparents were shipped off to the United States and South and Central America, as slaves. I had the opportunity to tour, preach and teach in several of the remote villages in and around Dakar.

I am fascinated with home mission and excited with the Foreign Mission Board's mission. We are commanded by Jesus to follow the Great Commission, "And he said unto them, Go ye into all the world, and preach the gospel to every creature." In 1996, the Emanuel Baptist Church was among the top five in leading the nation in foreign mission. In September 1998, we were listed as number two in giving to foreign mission. We continued in that category for many, many years. It becomes easier to give when you have observed firsthand the deplorable conditions under which many must live. After our visits, it ceased to be a burden and became a satisfaction to give.

In January 1999, at my request, President Henry J. Lyons appointed my wife, Flora D. Parker, an alternate delegate to the United Nations, to assist me in gathering materials for presentation to the convention. With her background in business and communications, she was of great assistance to me; attending weekly briefings, contacting representatives from the various departments of the NGO/DPI, and also facilitated my being able to work with these individuals. She was the cream in my coffee. We had the privilege of attending the Church Women's United Luncheon during its final meeting prior to the New Millennium. The honored guest for this luncheon was Mrs. Hillary Rodham Clinton.

In my fifth annual report, I reported on one of our most rewarding experiences; our visit to the Sandy Bay Community in St. Vincent, West Indies in April 1999, where I conducted a five-night preaching crusade. While conducting a crusade in Georgetown and the Sandy Bay village in St. Vincent, our contact person was Pastor Peter Ballantyne, pastor of the Sandy Bay Beach Gospel Chapel in the Village of Sandy Bay. Pastor Ballantyne is the representative of the Eastern Caribbean Garinagu for Christ Ministry in Sandy Bay. We discovered a dire need for our convention's presence in that region. As a church, the Emanuel Baptist Church of Elmont has undertaken the task of providing certain services that were of the utmost importance. Supplies, for schools and medical equipment for the Community Health Clinic there, have already been supplied. We will be returning to Sandy Bay to dedicate the supplies and equipment already sent. We sponsored a young lady, Samantha, for many years in high school, until graduation, and were happily informed about her recent marriage and work success. There is yet work to be done. I say to you wholeheartedly, it is more blessed to give than to receive.

Finally, I shall be working with the Honorable Henry Frank, executive director of the Haitian Centers Council in Brooklyn, New

York, to effectuate a cultural visit to Benin next August, providence prevailing. Let me say here that the United Nations continues to be the only peace-keeping agency in the Universe. Although it has not been able to achieve complete and lasting peace and, in my humble judgement, never will, nonetheless, the one and only machinery that man has devised to ensure some semblance of peace. Fragile though it may be, the United Nations has been able to keep the lid on major world conflicts.

In the Spirit of love, I served as United Nations representative from 1995 until 2000. It is my prayer that we will all seek God's guidance in all of our undertakings.

Mr. President, Members of the Board, and all who are present to share these precious moments with us, I leave you and this convention with this statement, as I conclude my fifth report. "Now to Him who is able to keep you from falling and to present you without blemish before the presence of His glory with rejoicing, to the only God, our Savior through Jesus Christ our Lord, be glory, majesty, dominion, and authority, before all time and now and forever." (And) Now may the God of peace who brought again from the dead our Lord Jesus, the Great Shepherd of the sheep, by the blood of the eternal covenant, equip you with everything good that you may do His will, working in you that which is pleasing in His sight, through Jesus Christ, to whom be glory forever and ever. Amen.

Chapter Nine

A LIFE OF SERVICE

1939 – Joined the CCC (Civilian Conservation Corps.) near Selma, Alabama. The site was known as "Alabama SP-10."

1942 – Sworn into the United States Army in Fort Bennings, Georgia

1945 – Enlisted in the United States Air Force.

1953 – United in Holy Wedlock to Willie Mae Bates of Hempstead. 1960 – Licensed to preach the Gospel of Christ at the Antioch Baptist Church, Hempstead, New York. And was later made assistant pastor; the only assistant pastor, at that time, in the history of churches.

1962 – Retired Master Sergeant from the United States Air Force.

1963 – Installed on February 17, 1963, as pastor of the Emanuel Baptist Church, becoming the fifth pastor in the history of the church. The church was located on Hendrickson and

Pelham Avenues with a membership of approximately sixty members. I challenged the people with the message, **"Give Me an Understanding Heart."**

1964 – Founded and organized the Jamaica Square Improvement League because of the need in the Elmont Community, and the concerns of the people in the area the Jamaica Square Area.

1967 – Awarded the Doctor of Divinity degree from the Detroit Baptist Seminary, Detroit, Michigan.

1974 – Was among the 6,500 recipients throughout the Free World to receive the "International Who's Who in Community Services" and was honored for four years as Community Leader of America. Served sixteen years as a Commissioner on the Board of Nassau County, Commission on Human Rights.

1976 – Installed on October 1, 1976 as the ninth moderator of the Eastern Baptist Association of New York, Inc. Because of my military training and discipline, I approached the task with profound determination. My inaugural address was delivered on October 1, 1976 at the Emanuel Baptist Church of Elmont, New York. My subject was, **"Give Me This Mountain."** During my four-year tenure, the association was led to pay off a mortgage indebtedness of $102,000 on the headquarters building on Kingston Avenue, Brooklyn, New York.

1979 – Appointed by Nassau County Executive Francis Purcell, as chairman of Nassau County Interracial Task Forces to deal with segregation and discrimination in the Nassau County Police Department and other agencies in the county.

1979 – Hosted "Morning Meditations" on Radio Station WTHE AM 150 in Mineola, New York, for thirty-four years. With the support of the Emanuel Baptist Church and the kind and generous support of my friends at the Carl C. Burnett Funeral Home; some 60,000 or more listeners were reminded daily that "No Day Is Well Spent Without a Talk with God."

1987 – Dedication of the New Emanuel Baptist Church on October 25, 1987, with a construction cost of $2.8 million.

1988 – Awarded the "Dr. Martin Luther King, Jr., Recognition Award" because of my concern in advancing the cause of people of color.

1989 – United in holy wedlock to the former Miss Flora D. Covington of Hollis, New York.

1991 – Elected as area vice president of the Empire Baptist Missionary Convention, serving the Long Island Shore Area, consisting of Nassau and Suffolk Counties.

1995 – Awarded the "New York State Black and Puerto Rican Ecumenical Service Award" for bridging the gap between various denominations.

1996 – Appointed United Nations Representative for our National Baptist Convention, USA, Inc., representing 8.5 million Baptists. Listed as one of the top Leaders, in financial support, to the National Baptist, Foreign Mission Board. Listed in the first Edition of, "Who's Who" in the National Baptist Convention, USA, Inc.

2001 – Witnessed the renaming of Hendrickson Avenue to read, "Rev. Dr. H. David Parker Avenue," on June 9, 2001. The town's political constituents, the Elmont Community, the Emanuel Baptist Church Family and friends were present. The Town of Hempstead wanted to leave a symbol of outstanding leadership and involvement in community activities. **"A Life Time Legacy!"**

2002 – Appointed president of the Board of Directors of the Montgomery Bible Institute and Theological Center in Montgomery, Alabama; the Reverend Dr. Willie L. Muse, founder and president. Because of my concern and support for education, honored with the title, Chairman Emeritus, of the Board of Directors.

2005 – Honored to be one of the recipients of the "Living Legends in Ministry Award" on May 21, 2005, for effective leadership, and as pastor and teacher. This award was presented by the Long Island Progressive Missionary Baptist Churches of the General Baptist Association of Long Island and Vicinity. Many pastors and friends witnessed this event.

2006 – Received the First "Rosa Parks Civil Rights Award," presented by the Town of Hempstead, on February 21, 2006.

2006 – Appointed in October 2006 as a member of the Advisory Board for the Empire Baptist Missionary Convention. After many years of service, hard work, sacrifice, dedication and commitment, I was frequently called upon for advice on solutions to problems.

2008 – Retired in March 2008, from the Emanuel Baptist Church after forty-five years of faithful service. Relocated to Baltimore, Maryland, with my lovely wife, Flora.

2009 – United on December 14, 2008, with the Rising Sun First Baptist Church, Baltimore, Maryland; under the leadership of Reverend Dr. Emmett C. Burns. Continued preaching the Good News of Christ. Honored with the title, Senior Associate Minister.

2011 – Celebrated my ninetieth birthday at Martin West, Baltimore, Maryland with a host of friends, far and near.

2014 – On November 16th, preached the Sermon (The Grip That Holds) at the Rising Sun First Baptist Church, Baltimore, Maryland

TO GOD BE THE GLORY,
FOR THE GREAT THINGS HE HAS DONE!!

Reverend Dr. Parker, drafted into the United States Army, and at the age of 21 years old, he had risen to the rank of Regimental Sergeant Major; the youngest in the entire United States Army to attain that rank.

Dr. Parker earned the Commendation Medal for Meritorious Service as a Military Historical Writer and Public Relations Specialists

In 1959, Dr. Parker was appointed assistant to the pastor of the
Antioch Baptist Church of Hempstead and served four years. In
1963, he was called to the Emanuel Baptist Church of Elmont,
New York; there were only sixty members at that time. During
his first eighteen months as pastor, 126 persons were added to the
membership.

Dr. Parker organized the Jamaica Square Improvement League, designed to deal with the problems that confronted African Americans and children in the community. He was concerned about the young and the aged. He made unannounced visits to schools, community events; he was highly respected by the Elmont and Hempstead Community.

Reverend Dr. H. David Parker received many noteworthy awards. Because of his effective leadership as pastor and teacher, he was one of the recipients of the "Living Legends in Ministry Award, and awarded the First "Rosa Parks Civil Rights Award

Jesus said, "Go ye therefore, and teach all nations, baptizing them in the name of the Father, **and** of the Son, **and** of the Holy Ghost: Teaching them to observe all things, whatsoever, I have commanded you; and lo, I am with you always even unto the end of the world." (Matthew 28:19, 20)

Because of Dr. Parker's effective leadership and involvement in community activities, the Town of Hempstead wanted to leave a symbol of his commitment. Family and friends witnessed the renaming of Hendrickson Avenue to read "Rev. H. David Parker Avenue."

Because of Dr. Parker's foresight, and humanitarian services, Emanuel was a beacon in the Elmont Community.

Dr. Parker retired March 2008, after serving forty-five years at Emanuel, with a membership of approximate 750 members. He and his wife, Flora, relocated to Baltimore, Maryland.

Chapter Ten

WORDS OF WISDOM

To The Young Ministers of the Gospel

"For I am not ashamed of the gospel of Christ: for it is the power of God unto salvation to everyone that believeth; to the Jew first, and also to the Greek."
(Romans 1:16)

"The good news of Jesus Christ is more than facts to be believed; it is also a life to be lived, a life of righteousness befitting the person, justified freely by God's grace through the redemption that is in Christ Jesus." This is my understanding from the beginning of my ministry.

In 1955, I was counting the years before retirement from the Air Force into civilian life. I thought I would find a job in public service and could live fairly comfortably with my pension. But the Lord moves in mysterious ways. One night as I lay in bed, in a semiconscious state, I saw myself in the wilderness preaching. The harder I tried to escape, and the people tried to hush me, the more I would preach. I remember running up mountains and into valleys, trying to get away, but everywhere I turned, I saw an open Bible. "I knew God had called me. I began to study the Bible intensely to prepare for the ministry." Four years from the date of this dream, I was ordained to preach the Gospel of Christ.

Because of the grace of God, I have been in the ministry now fifty-one years, preaching, teaching and encouraging God's people. In my many years of praying, meditating, and preaching, I am confident that I can share a little information about leading the flock (the sheep and the shepherd). It has been many years now since, in a little wooden church in the rural area of Alabama, that I was chosen by God to walk humbly, live justly and to love mercy. Now, as I am guided by His righteous hand, I am always conscious of my role and responsibility in ministry. My top priority is to preach what thus saith the Lord.

In my earlier years as a minister, never once did I maneuver my way to the front of the church, seeking recognition of man; it was more important to be asked up than to be asked down. I waited in the back of the church until I was called to the pulpit; yes, that was yesterday. Some may say "Old School." However, it worked for me; I am where I am today because of my diplomacy. I knew from an early age that the hand of the Lord was upon me, guiding and directing, and that in due time, He would fulfill His purpose in my life. I am standing on His promise. "But they that wait upon the Lord shall renew their strength; they shall mount up with wings as eagles; they shall run, and not be weary; and they shall walk, and not faint." (**Isaiah 40:31**) His word is true, yesterday, today, and forevermore. Amen.

Just remember, if God called you, He will place you in the right position, and in the right place at His appointed time. I beg you, stand still and wait on the Lord. Do not rush into the ministry with selfish motives, for fame, for fortune, because it may look glamourous. Make sure the voice that you hear is from the Lord. His word is clear, "Be not deceived; God is not mocked: for whatsoever a man soweth, that shall he also reap." (**Galatians 6:7**) God knows the heart; listen to His holy word, "Before I formed thee in the belly, I knew thee; and before thou camest forth out of the womb I sanctified thee, and I ordained thee a prophet unto the nations." (**Jeremiah 1:5**) With much emphasis, attending a college or university is excellent; however, do not attend school to become a minister; I was called by God first, after which, I attended school to strengthen my effort. "In all thy ways acknowledge him, and he shall direct thy paths." (**Proverbs 3:6**)

As preachers of the gospel of Jesus Christ, we are custodians of God's resources. Our task is to learn how to use them wisely. Pastors have the care of the flock committed to them by the Lord Jesus Christ. We must ever be concerned about the whole man. Not only must we take into account his spiritual needs, but his educational, economic, housing, and human rights needs. We must make our appeal for cooperation, sacrifice and concern on the basis of God's inspired Word. Jesus said, "For I was hungry, and you gave me no food; as thirsty, and ye gave me no drink; I was a stranger, and ye took me not in; naked and ye clothed me not; sick and in prison, and ye visited me not." We have a mandate from Him who called us as leaders of the flock.

During the forty-five years that I served as pastor of the Emanuel Baptist Church, I was not selfish; I was obedient to God's word. I listened and prayed for direction. When one of my sons/ministers was ready and prepared to move higher in his calling, and the Lord had blessed him in his effort, I was proud to support his assignment. I instruct them: as an ambassador of Christ, you are to preach and teach the uncontaminated doctrine of God's Word, administer the Sacraments according to Christ's institution, instruct the young, counsel the inquiring, care for the needy, minister to the dying, and pray for the spiritual welfare of every soul under your care. I always make myself available to the young minister or pastor who is trying to walk worthy of his calling.

I am happy to repeat, again, that I had the privilege of installing five ministers who are proclaiming the Gospel of Christ; namely, Reverend Willie Belcher, First Baptist Church, Cutchogue, Long Island; Reverend Charles Ancrum, Antioch Baptist Church, Jamaica, New York; Reverend Reginald Lewis, Liberty Grove Baptist Church,

Taylorsville, North Carolina; Reverend Kent Edmondson, Mt. Olive Baptist Church, Oyster Bay, Long Island; and Reverend Donald Butler, Community Baptist Church, Southampton, LI, New York. I also licensed two; Reverend Ronald Simpkins, Freewheel Baptist Church, Jamaica, New York; and my son, Minister David Parker. I pray that all senior pastors will develop this relationship with their spiritual sons/son. It is truly a blessing to have a father and son relationship. There is not room for jealousy or envy because of the progress that one is making in his own mission; there is always room for growth. Help him, support him, and always offer your support. My strength and blessings come from being around and encouraging young ministers to keep striving for the work of the kingdom.

As Paul encouraged his son, Timothy, I feel obligated to offer the same encouragement to the young preacher/minister of the Gospel today. Just a reminder, you are chosen by Jesus Christ, our Redeemer. Read daily His holy Word. Jesus said, "Ye have not chosen me, but I have chosen you, and ordained you, that ye should go and bring forth fruit, and that your fruit should remain; that whatsoever ye shall ask of the Father in my name, he may give it you" **(John 15:16).**

You are not doing God a favor by standing in the pulpit with a doleful expression, you are His anointed one; called to give the people an encouraging word from the Lord. This is not an easy task; this is an <u>uphill</u> journey. Lay aside all excuses: I am tired today; do not feel up to going; dragging in late; angry with the people, or

I have something else to do. I made my way to the house of wor-ship a many Sundays and days through the week that I did not feel well; but I made a promise to the Lord. Jesus said, "If any man will come after me, let him deny himself, and take up his cross daily, and follow me" (**Luke 9:23**). God prepares the called; therefore, let your conduct and attitudes exemplify the love of Christ at all times.

This is a serious assignment ordained by God; the pulpit is not a place to play, tell stories or show off, but is concentrated for the preaching of the gospel of Jesus Christ. Herewith, I began this dis-cussion from the words of God; starting with Romans the twelfth chapter, beginning at the first verse, Therefore, "I beseech you there-fore, brethren, by the mercies of God, that ye present your bodies a living sacrifice, holy, acceptable unto God, which is your reasonable service. And be not conformed to this world: but be ye transformed by the renewing of your mind, that ye may prove what is that good, and acceptable, and perfect, will of God." *This simply means that, by the grace and Spirit of God that is in you, you should put off con-cerning the former conversation of the old man, and be renewed in the spirit of your mind. Remember, you are not a newspaper reporter, nor a doorkeeper; you are God's representative in a confused and troubled world; a world that is bathing in sin, and needs leaders who will take a stand. There is no time to idle in wild conversation, filthiness, foolish talking, nor being, pompous and proud, but walk in love, as Christ also hath loved us. Put on the new man, which after God is created in righteousness and true holiness. Daily walk in godliness.*

As a minister of Christ, you are to devote yourself to the meditation and study of the Scriptures and carry out your duties in conformity with the Word of God. ...."For I say, through the grace given unto me, to every man that is among you, not to think more highly than he ought to think; but to think soberly, according as God hath dealt to every man the measure of faith." *There is no big me and little you in God's vineyard. Examine yourself every so often; see if you need a tune-up. We are called as ambassadors for Christ; to carry His message to a dying world. Our task, as it always has been, is to preach the Word with honesty and with a sense of urgency.* Paul states, "For though I preach the gospel, I have nothing to glory of: for necessity is laid upon me; yea, woe is unto me, if I preach not the gospel!" *(1 Corinthians 9:16)*

We are on the battlefield for the Lord; called to go where there is a need. He did not call us to sit high and look low; that is an honor that is given only to the Father. I say in all honesty, never feel as though you are too popular, sophisticated, educated, or important to provide service to the meek and lowly. Jesus stated, "They that be whole need not a physician, but they that are sick." (**Matthew 9:12**) "For as we have many members in one body, and all members have not the same office: So we, being many, are one body in Christ, and every one members one of another. Having then gifts differing according to the grace that is given to us, whether prophecy, let us prophesy according to the proportion of faith; Or ministry, let us wait on our ministering: or he that teacheth, on teaching; Or he that exhorteth, on exhortation: he that giveth, let him do it with simplicity; he that ruleth, with diligence; he that sheweth mercy, with cheerfulness." **(Romans 12:4-8)**

Strive to follow the example of Jesus the Christ, our Savior, and walk as an example to all believers in word, in love, in behavior and in the Holy Spirit; putting no stumbling block in anyone's path, so that the ministry will not be discredited. "Let love be without dissimulation. Abhor that which is evil; cleave to that which is good. Be kindly affectioned one to another with brotherly love; in honour preferring one another; Not slothful in business; fervent in spirit; serving the Lord; Rejoicing in hope; patient in tribulation; continuing instant in prayer; Distributing to the necessity of saints; given to hospitality. Bless them which persecute you; bless and curse not. Rejoice with them that do rejoice, and weep with them that weep. Be of the same mind one toward another. Mind not high things, but condescend to men of low estate. Be not wise in your own conceits. Recompense to no man evil for evil. Provide things honest in the sight of all men. If it be possible, as much as lieth in you, live peaceably with all men." **(Romans 12:9-18)**

By all means do not become comfortable and complacent in your own house of worship; expose your sheep to different cultures and experiences. A good leader always strives for the best for his followers. Most importantly, you are commanded to go and make disciples of all nations. The Lord's Holy Word teaches, "Go ye therefore, and teach all nations, baptizing them in the name of the Father, and of the Son, and of the Holy Ghost: Teaching them to observe all things whatsoever I have commanded you: and, lo, I am with you always, even unto the end of the world." (**Matthew 28:19-20**)

The young ministers face a heavy burden of responsibility in the churches today. All of the pastors who have been on the battlefield a long time (i.e., being in the ministry for thirty-five or forty years) are looked upon as somewhat old-fashioned. However, we have come this far by faith, leaning on the Lord for strength and guidance. I can say personally, the Lord has not failed me yet. We understand that the road is not easy, the task is challenging: false doctrine must be erased, public worship safeguarded, and mature leadership developed. Nevertheless, the conduct of the minister is a key component; you must be on guard at all times, lest your conduct become a liability, rather than an asset to the gospel. You must be careful to avoid false teachers and greedy motives, pursuing instead righteousness, godliness, faith, love, perseverance, and the gentleness that befits a man of God. We do not ever want to deflate our testimony in the church and community. The world is watching; they want to see a testimony as to who you are and whose you are. I encourage you, therefore, not to fall short of the expectations set before you. Walk daily with the Word of God. David states it clearly, "Thy word is a lamp unto my feet, and a light unto my path. (**Psalm 119:105**)

CALLED TO PREACH

The Undershepherd

H ear ye the Word from the Lord. "Before I formed thee in the belly, I knew thee, and ordained thee a prophet unto the nations." (**Jeremiah 1:5**) "For though I preach the gospel, I have nothing to glory of; for necessity is laid upon me; yea, woe is unto me, if I preach not the gospel." (**1 *Corinthians 9:16*)** "...And he said unto me, "Go ye into all the world, and preach the gospel to every creature." (**Mark 16:15**)

I stand in awe as I contemplate and reflect on the preacher's/ pastor's task. It is awe-inspiring, when taken seriously. As someone so aptly stated, one who preaches and pastors must be clear of his calling.

Permit me, if you will, to make one thing abundantly clear; at least to me. "God calls preachers, but He gives Pastors." There is a vast difference. For example, we see in Jonah 1:1-2 the call: "And the word of the Lord came unto Jonah saying, 'Arise, go to Nineveh, that great city, and cry against it; for their wickedness is come up before me.'" In Ezekiel 1:1, 4, again the call: "And he said unto me, Son of man, stand upon thy feet, and I will speak unto thee." "And he said unto me, son of Man, go, get thee unto the house of Israel, and speak with my words unto them." Paul bears out this fact in Romans 10:14, 15, when he questions the Roman Christians: "How, then, shall they call on him in whom they have not heard? And how shall they hear without a preacher. And how shall they preach except they be sent." *Paul poses four questions that require articulate and accurate answers.*

Yes, these divine words, we learn that God "calls" the preacher. What about the pastor? He "gives" pastors! To whom does He give them? To the Church! And what is the authority? **Ephesians 4:11, 12** declare, "And he gave some, apostles; and some, prophets; and some, evangelists; and some pastors and teachers. *The question may be asked, "Why did He (Christ) give these gifted individuals to the church?* **Ephesians 4:12**, "For the perfecting of the saints, for the work of the ministry, for the edifying of the body of Christ." (His Church)

My fifty-one years in ministry have given me the ability to warn others of the Preacher/Pastor Pitfalls: The preacher/pastor must ever approach his task with fear and trembling. He must realize that everyone who shakes his hand on Sunday morning is not his friend and that in his own strength he is a total failure. He must realize that he cannot compete with the secular world for recognition, that all of his help comes from God. He has no union to bargain for him. He has no guaranteed benefits from man; he must obey God. He must realize the he, like those around him, is imperfect. God's Word must be to him as in Jeremiah's heart, "like fire shut up in his bones." (Jeremiah 20:9)

His ultimate aim and purpose is to please God. I repeat, his task is an awesome one, and is not to be taken lightly. As stated by the

Apostle Paul, he has no alternative, but to preach. It is imperative! Necessity is laid upon him to preach and woe is unto him if he does not preach." (**1 Corinthians 9:16**)

Preaching is the minister's supreme task. The subject of Christian preaching is God and God's relationship to the world. Subjects like sociology, psychology, economic and political analysis, community affairs, and institutional promotions, if the minister is not careful, can become the functional center of the sermon. Where does this leave the wondering sinner? If the preacher/pastor is not careful, he will get caught up with causes rather than Christ: Drug abuse, AIDS, Crimes often time occupy far too much of the average minister's time. These are important topics, to be sure, but pastors are called, sent, and commissioned to preach God's eternal Word. To be sure, he must be concerned about drug abuse. He must be concerned about AIDS. He must be concerned about those elected to public office. He must be concerned about education; school board elections, but his primary purpose is the proclamation of the Gospel message.

When people seek legal advice, they go to an attorney. When they seek medical diagnosis, they go to a physician. When people seek an encounter with God, they come to the Church. The preacher/pastor is the theologian whose calling is to interpret the significance and the nature of God for the life of the world. Do not get entangled too deeply with the cares of this world. Paul had some specific instructions for young Timothy, when he said to him, "No man that warreth entangleth himself with the affairs of this life; that he may please him who hath chosen him to be a soldier." (**2 Timothy 2:4**)

I mentioned earlier in this discourse the pitfalls of the preacher/ pastor. Just to name a few: Seeking to be a superhuman. We are not Superman. The preacher/pastor is not perfect, although we expect him to be. He is a man with faults and failures. He will be tempted and tried the same as any other mortal. The pastor/preacher will make mistakes in judgment; seeking to please man, rather than God, is truly one of the major pitfalls to avoid. Striving to be popular = pitfall. Permitting accolades of fellow human beings to inflate your ego = pitfall. Acting as though you have the exclusive inter-pretation of God's Word = pitfall. Impatience, unteachable = pit-fall. Our calling as preachers demands that we seek, by earnest prayer, spiritual devotion, and a committed life, a special measure of divine aid to walk circumspectly before the world. Sobriety, moral strength, ethical insight, and spiritual power are required of every God-called preacher/pastor. It is imperative, therefore, that the preacher/pastor "Study to show himself approved unto God, a workman that needeth not to be ashamed, rightly dividing the word of truth." (**2 Timothy 2:15**)

It is a time for preaching, NOW; not playing or going through the motions. Paul predicted the coming apostasy. His instructions to his young son, Timothy are clear, "This know also, that in the last days perilous times shall come. For men shall be lovers of their own selves, covetous, boasters, proud, blasphemers, disobedient to parents, unthankful, unholy, Without natural affection, truce breakers, false accusers, incontinent, fierce, despisers of those that are good, Traitors, heady, high-minded, lovers of pleasures more than lovers of God; Having a form of godliness, but denying the power thereof: from such turn away." (**2 Timothy 3:1-5**)

"Yea, and all that will live godly in Christ Jesus shall suffer persecution. But evil men and seducers shall wax worse and worse, deceiving, and being deceived. But continue thou in the things which thou hast learned and has been assured of, knowing of whom thou hast learned them; And that from a child thou has known the holy scriptures, which are able to make thee wise unto salvation through faith which is in Christ Jesus. All scripture is given by inspiration of God, and is profitable for doctrine, for reproof, for correction, for instruction in righteousness, That the man of God may be perfect, thoroughly furnished unto all good works." (**2 Timothy 3:12-17**)

For a moment, let me speak to one of the old Patriarchs of the Old Testament. Brother Isaiah, speak to us. What is it that you wish to tell us about the preacher/ pastor, "Well, it was in the year that King Uzziah died I saw also the Lord sitting upon a throne, high and lifted up, and his train filled the Temple." What happened Isaiah? "Above it (the throne) stood the seraphim: How many were there? Apparently there were two of them, for one had six wings; he took two of them to coven his face; and he took two to cover his feet; and he used the other to fly. He said to the other seraphim,

"Holy, holy, holy, is the Lord of hosts: the whole earth is full of his glory." (**Isaiah 6:1-3**)

It is time for preaching the Gospel of Jesus Christ. *I close with these favorite scriptures,* Paul tells us in **2 Timothy 4:1-8,** "I charge thee therefore before God, and the Lord Jesus Christ, who shall judge the quick and the dead at his appearing and his kingdom: Preach the word; be instant in season, out of season; reprove, rebuke, exhort with all longsuffering and doctrine. For the time will come when they will not endure sound doctrine; but after their own lusts shall they heap to themselves teachers, having itching ears; But watch thou in all things, endure afflictions, do the work of an evangelist, make full proof of thy ministry."

What awaits the faithful preacher of righteousness? *Well now, the Lord has blessed me richly; I taught and preached what thus saith the Lord. I am now ninety-three years of age; the close of my ministry is near. I can joyfully say,* "For I am now ready to be offered, and the time of my departure is at hand. I have fought a good fight, I have finished my course, I have kept the faith: Henceforth, there is a crown of righteous laid up for me a crown of righteousness, which the Lord, the righteous judge, shall give me at that day and not to me only, but unto all them also that love his appearing. Do thy diligence to come shortly unto me." (**2 Timothy 4:1-9**) *Preach the word.*

Keep the faith! May the Lord Jesus Christ be with you always. Amen.

Chapter Eleven

THE PREACHED WORD

"A GREAT NATION"
(Galatians 5:13, 14)

As I was searching my library for additional information to include in this book, I came across a sermon that I preached at the Emanuel Baptist Church on Sunday, July 4, 1976, just three months prior to being installed as the **sixth moderator** of the Eastern Baptist Association of New York, Incorporated. The subject of this sermon: **"A Great Nation."** Additional scriptural references will be used in this presentation.

"For, brethren, ye have been called unto liberty; only use not liberty for an occasion to the flesh, but by love serve one another. For all the law is fulfilled in one word, even in this: Thou shalt love thy neighbor as thyself."

And now I quote the message with some modification. It begins thusly: "We might well begin our message by saying, 'Happy

Birthday; America!' And today, we are joined in this observance to celebrate the 200 birthday of this nation, which we call America. Today, we are joined in this observance by free men and women the world over. And I think it is worth noting that July 4th, the exact date of our beginning, falls on Sunday this year. Could it be that God has so ordained it that we, Americans, might return to Him and to the principles that made this nation great if, indeed, she is great?

More than six months ago, a slogan began to appear across this nation proclaiming, "The Spirit Of 76." I trust that we will not allow this slogan to mar our view of the true Spirit – The Spirit Of Christ! I believe that America today holds a unique place in history; for the world looks to her for leadership. I trust that this leadership will be in a direction that leads back to God, and the great Christian principles upon which this nation was founded.

Permit me, if you will, to share with you several passages from the Old Testament: I begin with the Patriarch Moses. Moses recounts here his experiences with God on Mt. Sinai. In that eighth chapter of the book of Deuteronomy, Moses spoke to Israel in these words: "Therefore thou shalt keep the commandments of the LORD thy God, to walk in his ways, and to fear him. For the LORD thy God bringeth thee into a good land, a land of brooks of water, of fountains and depths that spring out of valleys and hills; A land of wheat, and barley, and vines, and fig trees, and pomegranates; a land of oil olive, and honey; A land wherein thou shalt eat bread without scarceness, thou shalt not lack any thing in it; a land whose stones are iron, and out of whose hills thou mayest dig brass. When thou hast eaten and art full, then thou shalt bless the LORD thy God for the good land which he hath given thee. Beware that thou forget not the LORD thy God, in not keeping his commandments, and his judgments, and his statues, which I command thee this day: Lest when thou hast eaten and art full, and hast built goodly houses, and dwelt therein And when thy herds and thy flocks multiply and thy silver and thy gold is multiplied; Then thine heart be lifted up, and thou forget the LORD thy God, which brought thee forth out of the land of Egypt, from the house of bondage; Who led thee through that great and terrible wilderness, wherein were fiery serpents, and scorpions, and drought, where there was no water; who brought thee forth water out of the rock of flint; Who fed thee in the wilderness with manna, which thy fathers knew not, that he might humble thee, and that he might prove thee, to do thee good at thy latter end; (And thou say in thine heart, My power and the might of mine hand hath gotten me this wealth.) But thou shalt remember the LORD thy God: for it is he that giveth thee power to get wealth, that he may establish his covenant which he sware unto thy fathers, as it is this day." **Deuteronomy 8:6-18**)

As Moses continued to appeal to God on the behalf of Israel, as recorded in that **ninth chapter of Deuteronomy,** God responded to Moses' plea in **Deuteronomy 9:14.** Here are His words: "Let me alone, that I may destroy them, and blot out their name from under heaven: and I will make of thee a nation mightier and greater than they."

As we consider God's mercy as He dealt with His children, David reminds us in **Psalm 33:12** of the mercy that God showers upon His obedient children, "Blessed is the nation, whose God is the LORD." Solomon, that man of wisdom, encourages us with these words. He said, "Righteousness exaltcth a nation, but sin is a reproach to any people."

What is it that makes a nation great? Is it the size of that nation? Is it the wealth of that nation? Is it the technology of that nation? Is it the proficiency of that nation? Is it the military power of that nation? Just what makes a nation great?

If we were to consider two nations; Ancient Greece and Palestine, we would discover that neither one of them could be classified great by today's standards. Yet, they were great. Note, if you will, their contributions to the world's community. Greece gave to the world philosophy and the appreciation of beauty. Ancient Palestine gave to the world the knowledge of God, and man's place in the Universe. That made them great, despite the fact that they were not privileged to be great in size, possessed of wealth, technology, proficiency, nor military power. But they were great, and history will attest to that fact.

The question becomes, "What makes a nation great?" What makes America great? Certainly we have size. We have technology. We have proficiency. We have wealth. We have military power. The standard of living that this nation enjoys is a utopia, a dream, unbelievable to the rest of the world.

I would pose another question: "What makes America great?" I believe that when all of the patriotic rhetoric has been said and forgotten, we must conclude that her "faith in spiritual values" is the one thing that makes her great! The founders of this nation, and we were there, believed that above the material things of life, there were ultimately more important values. "Man does not live by bread alone."

Our great ideals are rooted in our Christian heritage. In retrospect, if we look at the root age of each of our great ideals, we will find at the root some great Christian convictions. But today, we must ask ourselves this question: "Will these ideals be able to live on when they are cut off from their roots?" A cut flower will live on for a while, but eventually it must fade away.

As I hasten to a close, I share again my concern that there may come into being more and more of a spiritual vacuum among mankind. When man drives out religion, something else will come up from the drain. We must stand fast by our Christian heritage and Christian ideals. Let us never forget the edit of the ancient writer, "Blessed is the Nation whose God is the Lord." As we recount the past, and contemplate the future, let us hold fast to the profession of our faith, without wavering. And may we never forget that "Righteousness exalts a Nation; but sin is a reproach to any people."

You may ask yourself this question, on the occasion of America's 200th birthday: "What does America need? What do we, as individuals, need?" And I believe a succinct answer to these questions is: **(a)** America does not need more material development; America needs more spiritual development. **(b)** America does not need more intellectual power; America needs more moral power. **(c)** America does not need more knowledge; America needs more character. **(d)** America does not need more government; America needs more spiritual culture. **(e)** America does not need more law; America needs to show more love. **(f)** America does not need more of the things that are seen; America needs more of the things that are unseen.

There are some basic convictions that we should forever hold and cherish. Known as the **"Declaration of Independence,"** they were handed down by the Founders of this nation and dated July 4, 1776. I quote for you now this important document:

"When in the Course of human events, it becomes necessary for one people to dissolve the political bands which have connected them with another, and to assume among the powers of the earth, the separate and equal station to which the Laws of Nature and of Nature's God entitle them, a decent respect to the opinions of mankind requires that they should declare the causes which impel them to separation.

"We hold these truths to be self-evident, that all men are created equal, that they are endowed by their Creator with certain

unalienable Rights that among these are Life, Liberty and the pursuit of Happiness. That to secure these rights, Governments are instituted among Men, deriving their just Powers from the consent of the governed,—-That whenever any Form of Government becomes destructive of these ends, it is the Right of the People to alter or to abolish it, and to institute new Government, laying its foundation on such principles and organizing its powers in such form, as to them shall seem most likely to affect their Happiness. Prudence, indeed, will dictate that Governments long established should not be changed for light and transient causes; and accordingly all experience hath shewn, that mankind are more disposed to suffer, while evils are sufferable, than to right themselves by abolishing the forms to which they are accustomed. But when a long train of abuses and usurpations, pursing invariably the same Object evinces a design to reduce them under absolute Despotism, it is their right, it is their duty, to throw off such Government, and to provide new guards for their future security—-Such has been patient sufferance of these Colonies; and such is now the necessity which constrains them to alter their former Systems of Government. The history of the present King of Great Britain is a history of repeated injuries and usurpations, all have in direct object the establishment of an absolute Tyranny over these States. To prove this, let facts be submitted to a candid world."

Friends, we must maintain faith in a Divine Creator, i.e., God. We must maintain faith in a moral order of the Universe; **faith** that

justice and **righteousness** will have a better chance in the courts of our land, when we stick hard by our Christian ideals.

Moses, as you spoke to Israel, may these words be appropriate for us today, even under the dispensation of grace. You warned Israel with these words from **Deuteronomy 8:6-18.**

I repeat again, with much emphasis. As we consider God's mercy as He dealt with His children, David reminds us in **Psalm 33:12** of the mercy that God showers upon His obedient children. That verse reads, "Blessed is the nation whose God is the LORD." Solomon, that man of great wisdom, encourages us with these words. He said, "Righteousness exalteth a nation, but sin is a reproach to any people."

Yes, God is on our side. If we obey Him by following His word, if we place our faith in His Son, the Lord Jesus Christ, if we cast all of our cares upon Him, He will see us through. That is why I sing sometime, "I Am Happy With Jesus Alone."

#2

A More Excellent Way

1 Corinthians 13

The foundation for 1 Corinthians Chapter 13 is found in 1 Corinthians 12:28-31. "And God hath set some in the church: first apostles, second prophets, third teachers; after that miracles, then gifts of healing, helps, governments, diversities of tongues. Are all apostles? Are all prophets? Are all teachers? Are all workers of miracles? Have all the gifts of healing? Do all speak with tongues? Do all interpret? But covet earnestly the best gifts; and yet show I unto you **a more excellent way."**

The question: "What is this thing called '**Love'?**" Why is it the strongest force that permeates man's total being? Why did the Apostle Paul give such prominence to this virtue or this way? I think we can answer that by saying that "God Is Love!"

The Apostle John affirms this fact when he declared in 1 John 4:8, "He that loveth not knoweth not God; for God is love." This same John goes on to make this profound pronouncement: "And we (the Believers) have known and believe the love that God hath to us. God is Love, and he that dwelleth in love dwelleth in God and God in him." This statement should satisfactorily answer the question as to why Paul gave such prominence to this idea of love. It is because God is love.

What is this thing called love? As I search God's Word, I am convinced that love is the personification of godliness, and the embodiment of all that is enshrined in God's being. I need to remind us that love is more than a feeling of endearment. In reality, love expresses the essential nature of God. Love can only be known by the action that it produces. The perfect example of this fact is when God gave His only begotten Son for the salvation of the world. (**John 3:16**) This verse is one of the most popular verses in the New Testament. "For God so loved the world that He gave His only begotten Son, that whosoever believeth in Him should not perish, but have everlasting life." When we search the record we will discover that the Apostle Paul had no difficulty in correcting the Corinthian Christians for their lack of understanding of the "**More Excellent Way**." As many modern-day Christian, they were caught up in their own special gifts and interests, and were neglecting or misunderstanding the true concepts of love. They flaunted their air of superiority, especially the "tongue-talkers." The Apostle Paul said to them, in effect, covet (or cherish) earnestly the best gifts (healing, helps, governments, diverse tongues, or whatever) that you may have, but I will show you a better way; or a more excellent way...**LOVE**.

My friends, take comfort! I sincerely believe this one thing and that is, "Love can overcome most, if not all, of life's difficulties." When we resolve in our minds that there is no way, absolutely no way, to bypass love, to overcome love, to subdue love, or to defeat love, then we must trust God's Word. According to the record, love is able to bear all things; love is able to believe all things; love hopes all things, and love endures all things. It is no wonder, then, that Paul declared that love would never fail.

Consider with me these four aspects of love. May we consider what they are able to accomplish. These aspects of love enable the believer, as well as the unbeliever, to see love under its widest scope. It is impossible to escape the opportunities offered, except by outright refusal and rejection. I might add here that I believe that there are those who do not desire the gracious benefits that love offers. The reason being, they reject Him who personifies genuine love, and that man is Jesus.

For a few minutes, let us scrutinize these four aspects of love. What do they ensure? Analyze carefully that seventh verse of the thirteenth chapter of 1 Corinthians. What does it say about love? **It Beareth all Things**. That phrase, "bears all things," is best translated "covers all things." For example, a tiny grain of sand will irritate the flesh of an oyster, becoming a painful, agonizing nuisance. But a substance within the oyster's body is wrapped around the tiny grain of sand that produces the pain. The end result is that a beautiful pearl is formed. Love does the same with the forces of evil. A substance within the heart of the beloved hides or covers the ugliness of opposition. It does it with care, compassion and concern. It is seen as redemption that produces change and commitment. The citizens in India saw it in Mahatma Gandhi. America and the world saw it in Martin Luther King, Jr. Centuries ago, it was manifested to the Jews, Greeks, and Romans by Jesus, the Christ. It was strong and powerful then and even today. We are able to see it, feel it, and experience the love of Christ. No wonder Isaiah says, "Surely, our grief he himself bore, and our sorrows he carried." (**Isaiah 53:4**)

Love Believes All Things. It believes in the individual; their strength and their weaknesses. Love believes in the maximum, yet, it encourages those who only aspire for the minimum. Love believes in accomplishments, not failures. Here is a true example: **Abraham** believed that there was a city whose builder and maker was God. He believed so strongly that he started searching for that city, not knowing where he was going. **Elisha** believed, for he proclaimed to the children of God one day, "Those who are with us are more than those who are with them." (**2 Kings 6:16**) Job believed, for he said one day, in the throes of despondency, "though he slay me, yet will I trust in Him. All the days of my appointed time will I wait, until my change comes."

Love Hopes All Things: Look at the record. Hope takes a sunny and cheerful view of self, others, the world, and God. Why? Because hope is inspired by love. After the shepherds got a glimpse of Jesus in the manger, they departed with hope. When the wise men saw the bright star in the east, they began their journey in hope. **Simeon** was given hope when he held the baby Jesus in the temple and spoke these immortal words of comfort: "Now Lord, thou dost let thy bond-servant depart in peace, according to thy word; for my eyes have seen thy salvation, which thou hast prepared in the presence of all people, a light of revelation to the Gentiles, and the glory of thy people, Israel." (Luke 29-32) The **prodigal son** was given hope in the pig pen, when he came to himself.

I need to remind us that when faith loses its grip, as it sometimes does, love will still endure. When hope gives out, love endures. Love transcends all barriers; love overcomes all hindrances and obstacles. Love overcomes all pitfalls; love is a bridge over deep waters. When **Isaiah** brought **Hezekiah** that disturbing message of his impending death, he endured and lived another fifteen years. **Elijah** endured the threats of Jezebel's messages. Jesus warned His disciples that they would be hated of all men for His name's sake, but if they endure to the end, they would be saved. (**Matthew 10:22**)

Well, why are these four aspects of love so important to us? I believe that we can be assured that love is able to bear all things, to believe all things, to hope in all things, and to endure all things. Again, the question may be asked, why? The answer is simple: because Jesus Christ is the perfect example and the personification of love. He bore the ridicule of an unfair trial; He endured the pain of a tortuous beating; He bore the agony and strain of carrying a heavy cross. But thank God, He defeated death with victorious and glorious resurrection. Praise the Lord!

As I consider what is known in the Christian circle, that thirteenth chapter of 1 Corinthians, as the "**Love Chapter**," I am convinced that love is the only way out for mankind. With all of the shortcomings of mankind, God, through His Son Jesus the Christ, still loves man. We take comfort in the fact that Christ believed in man and that man was redeemable. Christ believed that man could be reconciled to His Father, and that is why He was willing to lay down His life for mankind. Christ deemed man worthy to be saved and what did He do? He showed man the love side. Christ paid the price; He was willing to stand His bond, placing all of His earthly possessions up for collateral: His own life. By taking that position, Christ saw love at its very best.

The rich young ruler could have been saved, but his "love value" was misdirected. He loved his goods more than he did his Christ. In so doing, he forfeited his rights to become an eternal kingdom dweller. Christ had hoped that lost man would accept His love and be retrieved; like the woman caught in the very act of adultery. As I look at this love, I am compelled to make these observations. I am convinced that all I need and all you need is: His grace to hold me securely; His light to show me the way; His love to bind me always; His strength for every day's journey; His power to give me courage; His wisdom to guide me; His mercy for my sinfulness; and His benevolence to supply my every need.

So my dear friends, here I stand today, seeking to fully understand love. The text states the four aspects of love, but the context tells us far more. It tells us that love suffereth long; it is kind; it envieth not; vaunteth not itself; not easily provoked; thinks no evil; doth not behave herself unseemly, seeketh not her own; is not happy with that which is wrong; happy with the truth. Loves does not fail. The other gifts will fail one day, but love will endure.

#3

"BENT BUT NOT BROKEN"
2 Corinthians 12:7-10

Today I want to deal with the Apostle Paul, whose life experiences were similar to Job's.

"And lest I should be exalted above measure through the abundance of the revelations, there was given to me a thorn in the flesh, the messenger of Satan to buffet me, lest I should be exalted above measure. For this thing I besought the Lord thrice, that it might depart from me. And he said unto me, 'My grace is sufficient for thee: for my strength is made perfect in weakness. Most gladly therefore will I rather glory in my infirmities, that the power of Christ may rest upon me. Therefore I take pleasure in infirmities, in reproaches, in necessities, in persecutions, in distresses for Christ's sake: for when I am weak, then am I strong."

In Paul's second letter to the church members at Corinth, "But to keep me from being puffed up with pride because of the many wonderful things I saw, I was given a painful physical ailment, which acted as Satan's messenger to beat me and keep me from being proud. Three times I prayed to the Lord about this and asked him to take it away. But His answer was 'My grace is all you need, for my power is greatest when you are weak,' I am most happy, then, to be proud of my weaknesses, in order to feel protection of Christ's power over me. **(10)** I am content with weaknesses, insults, hardships, persecutions, and difficulties for Christ's sake. For when I am weak, then I am strong." (2 **Corinthians 12:7-10; GNB-TEV**)

Notice the similarities between Job and Paul. I begin this message today, Father's Day, by stating, emphatically, that no one cherishes suffering. It would seem that Paul's statement about glorying in afflictions runs counter with man's true nature. I am convinced that no one rushes out to invite pain, woes, and suffering. So the Apostle Paul, even though he was Christian, sought relief from his afflictions. It is man's nature to seek relief from his sufferings, in whatever form. But through his affliction, he was taught a great lesson by the Great Physician, Jesus Christ, who comforted Paul with these words, "My Grace Is Sufficient!" It is God's grace that sustains us.

After Christ had assured Paul that His grace was sufficient, Paul was then able to say, "Most gladly therefore will I rather glory in my infirmities, that the power of Christ may rest upon me." Paul went on to say, "Therefore, I take pleasure in infirmities, in reproaches, in necessities, in persecutions, in distresses." And the question you may ask: why? And the answer, "For Christ's sake: for when I am weak, then am I strong." (**2 Corinthians 12:9-10**) These should be comforting words for all of us, when we must deal with our adversities.

Christians should be the happiest, most contented people in the Universe, when they have the assurance that God's grace is sufficient. It is said that gloom and happiness flow more from one's inner self than from external happiness and conditions. Identically, the same situation will release gloom in one person and happiness in another. It may be safely assumed that for some folk, when difficulties arise, they are ready to capitulate and even, for some, commit suicide. While others may experience the same difficulty or will pray, sing or laugh away their troubles. The relationship with Christ is the determinant factor.

To be sure, all of us meet difficulty at one time or another. No one is exempt from difficulty. Often times we ponder our predicament and conclude that ours is the toughest and most stabbing of all plights. But we must always remember that this same Paul declared to the Corinthian believers that "No temptation hath taken you but such as is common to man: but God is faithful, who will not suffer you to be tempted above that ye are able; but will with the temptation also make a way to escape, that ye may be able to bear it." **(1 Corinthians 10:13).** Often times we will move around grumbling, with our spirits drooped.

There is an answer to this condition. The Bible instructs us to "Cast all of our cares upon Him, for He does care for us." **(1 Peter 5:7)** Too often we are tempted to conclude that John Jones or Mary Jane is better than we are. They are rich! They have it soft. They own a big business. They are prosperous. But do not worry about John Jones or Mary Jane, they have difficulties, too. Settling our difficulties is not dependent upon standing in the shoes of another person, when they do not fit our feet. Our determination should be to make capital of the difficulty in which we find ourselves.

Finding himself with a thorn in the flesh, Paul prayed for relief; a natural instinct. He prayed once; he prayed the second time; and he prayed the third time. He was persistent, as all believers should be. He received an answer but not as he thought or desired. Often times our prayers are not answered as we expect them to be. We expect God to come one way, but He comes in another. As Elijah stood on the mountain, the mighty wind rent and broke the mountain open. After the wind, then came earthquake. But Jehovah was not in the quake. After the trembling, the fire, but the mighty God was not in the fire. After the fire, came a still, small voice and that small voice brought God's message to Elijah. Elijah had expected to find God in the wind, the earthquake, and the fire, but He came the unexpected way...in the still, small voice.

Often times we expect God to come by land and He comes by water. Paul prayed for the removal of the thorn in his flesh. He expected that it would be removed. But not so! God did something even better for Paul. God gave him the comforting assurance that regardless of the difficulties, "My grace is sufficient." My un-merited favor is sufficient. Instead of the thorn being extracted, it was used as a spur. "My power is made perfect in weakness." Difficulties give religion, Christian religion, the opportunity for which it asks. The Christian religion specializes in the impossible. When we come to that deep chasm, deep and wide, religion, Christian religion, becomes that strong bridge. When we come to a mountain steep and rough, it makes of us Alpine climbers. When we are passing through the valley, it makes of death a shadow. I'm talking about Christian religion. A fiery furnace, a jail, a dungeon, slavery, a cross, give religion a dark background against which it sparkles.

The need of religion sprouts in difficulty. Difficulty is often used as an excuse for not doing what we should do. The slightest pebble becomes a stumbling block over which many of us fall; to which attached; under which we lie, behind which we hide. Many of us view our excuses through high-powered magnifying glasses. Moles hills become mountains; twigs become giant oaks. The exaggeration complex has bewitched us. In a split second, we can manufacture the smoothest alibi or make a series of excuses as high and huge as the Rocky Mountains. Make an excuse for someone else, never make an excuse for yourself. Instead of allowing a difficulty to be a millstone, use that difficulty to pave the highway over which to travel. Given a task to perform, many of us will begin to multiply reasons why we cannot live up to our potential.

Difficulties are indigenous to and contingent upon us. They are as large or small as we permit them to be. Prior to taking possession of a new territory promised by God, twelve men, one from each of the twelve tribes of Israel, were sent to view the land; size up the situation, tabulate the strength of the opposition and to report back to the leader. These twelve men went to the same place; saw the same people, encountered the same difficulty. Ten of them reported,

"They are giants, and we are as grasshoppers in their sight." Two of them, however, Joshua and Caleb, submitted a minority report, after seeing the land, the same people, and same difficulties. They said, "Let us go up AT ONCE and possess the land; God has promised it." He has kept every promise that He has ever made. We are well able to overcome it."

Someone has said that Opposition Provides Opportunity. The human spirit responds to challenge. It is so constituted that it will not take a dare. Life may pinch us with the grip of a vice, but there is something in the best of us which whispers, "Buckle up," "Hold Out," "Hold On!"

A story is told that some years in Chicago, one of Chicago's leading newspapers, the *Chicago Tribune,* carried a story of a woman who lived in that city. The story read, and I quote it here: "She has been ill for twenty-five years. She has had thirteen major operations; she has been to the hospital thirty-three times. Her body has wasted to seventy pounds. Her hair is now snow white. All of her teeth were removed eight years ago. The muscles of her throat are closed so tightly that not a tiny tube could be inserted for liquid feeding. Her legs have become so weak that they fail to support the weight of her thin body, so that she crawls on her knees. She has been both thirsty and hungry for seven years. She is fed by shots of Ovaltine and Malted milk. She has never been on relief nor asked for outside help. She supports herself and until a few months ago, she also cared for her mother. She does delicate baby clothing and embroidery. Her eyes have been weakened by illness, but she uses both glasses and magnifying glasses. Her room and person are immaculate. She is **Cheerful, Hopeful, and Happy** and smiles at the sad plight of her life." Her case is second only to Job's" What a story! Could you have taken what she endured?

As I hasten on, may I suggest to all of us to never worry about difficulties or handicaps. Thank God for them and especially if you are a child of God. Remember Jesus and His cross. An apple tree yields its best fruit when gashed. A finished musician can sing his sweetest songs when wounded. A Christian pure and undefiled can pray best when in trouble. Do not worry about the vast host of the Midianites, thank God for Gideon's army. Don't worry about the storms of life, thank God for Him who can speak and cause the winds and waves to obey His will. Do not worry about the thorn in the flesh. Thank God that His grace is sufficient. Do not worry about treachery. Thank God for the redemptive plan of salvation. Do not worry about your weakness. Thank God that He uses the weak to confound the mighty.

Action under fire is the surest index as to the basic ingredient of what strong men are made of. What one does in a crisis proves what he is. A man who cries in a crisis cannot be trusted. One who complains in a crisis is a grumbler. One who shifts the blame in crisis is an imposter. One who gives up in a crisis is a quitter. One who grabs the steer by the horns is a master. He who can smile, be patient, work as though all things depended on him and pray as though all depended on God, is a conqueror.

Can you recall any person who had more acute difficulties than Jesus? He had a lost world to be redeemed by a plan of salvation; twelve un-learned men with whom to organize His church; among them a doubter, a traitor, and a denier or liar; no temple in which to preach, for they drove Him out of the synagogue when He uttered these words, "The Spirit of the Lord is upon me;" no home in which to live. For He said, "The birds have nests, the foxes have holes, but the Son of Man hath no place to lay His head." He was without the sanction of Jewish tradition and the Mosaic Law, for He said, "You have heard it said of old 'An eye for an eye and a tooth for a tooth,' but I say if your enemy smites you on one cheek turn him the other also."

Now we hear Him in these words, "My Grace is sufficient for thee; for my strength is made perfect in weakness." (2 Corinthians 1:1-10) Paul, I know the thorn in the flesh is annoying, but God's grace is sufficient.

#4

"COUNTING THE COST"
(The Duties of the Deacon)
Acts 6:1-8

The Word of the Lord, "And in those days, when the number of the disciples was multiplied, there arose a murmuring of the **Grecians** against the **Hebrews,** because their widows were neglected in the daily ministration. Then the twelve called the multitude of the disciples unto them, and said, 'It is not fitting that we should leave the word of God, and serve tables. Wherefore, brethren, look among you for seven men of **honest report, full of the Holy Spirit and wisdom,** whom we may appoint over **this business.** But we will give ourselves **continually** to prayer, and to the ministry of the word.' And the saying pleased the **whole multitude**: and they chose **Stephen,** a man full of faith and the Holy Spirit, and **Phillip,** and **Prochorus,** and **Nicanor,** and **Timon,** and **Parmenas,** and **Nicolas,** a proselyte of Antioch, Whom they set before the apostles; and when they had prayed, they laid their hands on them. And the word of God increased, and the number of the disciples multiplied in Jerusalem greatly; and a great company of the priests were obedient to the faith. And Stephen, full of faith and power, did great wonders and miracles among the people." **(Acts 6:1-8)**

Now look at **(Acts 7:59-60)** "And they stoned Stephen, calling upon God, and saying, Lord Jesus, receive my spirit. And he kneeled down, and cried with a loud voice, Lord; lay not this sin to their charge. And when he had said this, he fell asleep."

Permit me to say at the outset that there has long been confusion about the role of the deacon as it relates to his duties in the local church. I want to suggest to our friend, and brethren, that you study carefully the scripture references that I have shared with us today. There are numerous books that have been written by authors who have not experienced one day as a pastor. Permit the Bible to be your source.

Since the Baptist church has its own Sovereign Power, i.e., power within itself, it has the sole responsibility for the training, motivating, and inspiring of its own members. No external force or guidance is required. Most of Paul's epistles, if not all of them, would not have been written had it not been for the church.

In light of the inspired Scripture, it is well to determine if the deacon today is giving to the church what the church requires and deserves of him, and whether the church is doing likewise by the deacon. We need to recognize that the requirement is reciprocal. And I need to say at the outset that this message is not designed or intended as a public censure or ridicule of the deacon, but rather to emphasize the deacon's role in the local church in light of God's Word. Because deacons are publicly set aside by the church they have a right to know what is expected of them by the church.

The question may be asked: **What Is A Deacon?** There may be several interpretations. But the most accepted one is the original

Greek interpretation, **"Diak-onos.** This simply means that: He is a servant; he is a helper; he is a teacher; he is an aid to the pastor; he is the lesser of the two officers of the church, divinely sanctioned by the Holy Writ. It is to be emphasized here that the church really has only two officers: (1) the pastor. and (2), the deacon. And at this juncture I need to remind us that Christ did not require deacons; they came about after the Church had been established in Jerusalem shortly after the resurrection of Jesus Christ, and the descent of the Holy Spirit. and deacons were only required because of the tremendous growth of the Church, following the preaching of Deacon Stephen.

Permit me to share my convictions at this point, and I believe sanctioned by the Holy Writ. Deacons are not chosen to grace or beautify the church by their presence, or to lend prestige to some office of the Church. He is chosen because he is needed and there is work to do. The deacon should be the first person at the church when it is open. And remember, there was a time when the title "trustee," was not heard in the church. The duties that the trustees perform today were performed in those days by the deacons.

At the time written in our text, the Church at Jerusalem, during a sermon delivered by Peter, **Acts 2:41,** 3,000 persons united with the church. Shortly thereafter, following another sermon, 2,000 more received the word, believed and were baptized and added to the Church **(Acts 4:4).** And because of this exceeding growth, the apostles required assistance. The first deacons had power.

The question may be posed, "Why were they needed?" The answer: "To quiet a murmuring and unrest among the congregation." When the disciples multiplied in the Church, so did the unrest. No less true today! When church folk begin murmuring, it is a matter of serious concern. Of course, sometimes murmuring is done just to be contrary. But look at this situation here.

The apostles recognized that the **WORD** was the most important matter at the moment. Tables must be served, but **prayer** and the **Word** were far more important than serving tables. "The people are murmuring, but the murmuring is not sufficient reason to abandon the Word to become table waiters."

Observe the wisdom of these apostles. What did they do? They said to the people, "Look ye out among you; and select seven men whom we may appoint over this business…waiting tables." Do not look beyond your own congregation; among yourselves. They chose from among themselves; Grecians Jews; not Hebrew, but Grecian Jews. Why was it done in this manner? Because these were the ones that were being neglected!

Then, what are the qualifications of the deacon? They must be **MEN;** (repeat) of honest report; full of the Holy Ghost; and full of wisdom **(Acts 6:3)**. Observe if you will that **wisdom** comes after **Holy Ghost.** Man may possess an abundance of wisdom, knowledge, and intellect, but without the Holy Spirit, he is of little use in Christ's church. He must be full of the Holy Ghost. I would pose this question for your consideration: "Do the 20th & 21st Centuries churches insist on these qualifications?" Sadly, the answer is "No" in most instances. A good leader may be faithful in the church; may fulfill his obligations; may have many friends inside and outside of the church; may be well educated; having all of these desirable qualities, but, if he is not honest, full of the Holy Ghost, not full of wisdom; he is not qualified for the position of a deacon. These are the qualifications that Dr. Luke outlined for the deacon.

Now we take a look at what the Apostle Paul says about this position. Since the preacher and the deacon must be so closely allied and in harmony, Paul defined their duties with close similarity. Here is what he says in Scripture. Listen carefully to his words: "This is a true saying, If a man desire the office of a bishop, he desireth a good work." *(I need to say here and now that there is nothing improper with a desire to go higher, and especially in and for the cause of Christ.)* A bishop then must be blameless, the husband of one wife, temperate, sober-minded, of good behavior, given to hospitality, apt to teach; Not given to wine, not violent, not greedy of filthy lucre, but patient, not a brawler, not covetous; One that ruleth well his own house, having his children in subjection with all gravity (For if a man know not how to rule his own house, how shall he take care of the church of God?); Not a novice, lest being lifted up with pride he fall into the condemnation of the devil. Moreover, he must have a good report of them who are outside, lest he fall into reproach and the snare of the devil. *Now listen to this:* In like manner must the deacon be grave, not double-tongued, *(that is, talking out of both size of the mouth)* not given to **much wine,** not greedy of filthy lucre, Holding the mystery of the faith in a pure conscience. And let these first be proved; then let them use the office of a deacon, being found blameless." **(1 Timothy 3:1-13)**

The apostles advised the congregation to look among themselves and choose seven men. The apostles did not take it upon themselves to arbitrarily select these seven men; they permitted the congregation to make the choice and that suggestion pleased the whole multitude. And what did they do? They chose Stephen, full of faith and the Holy Ghost; Philip, Prochorus, Nicanor, Timon, Parmenas, Nicolas. These men must have shown great promise and faithful service to be selected out of such a great multitude. The multitude then set these seven men before the apostles and when they had prayed, they laid their hands on them. And what were the results of this action? Three important things took place: **(1)** The Word of God increased. **(2)** The number of disciples increased greatly in Jerusalem. **(3)** A great company of priests was obedient to the faith. We concluded my brothers and my sisters, that a deacon who meets these requirements is a great asset to the local church.

The divine and inspired record is that after the ordination or appointment, if you will, Stephen was full of faith and power, did great work; great wonders and miracles among the people. But what follows this action?

The record is that some of the Synagogue of the Libertines was disputing with Stephen but they could not resist his wisdom, because he was a man full faith and power. They recruited people to lie about him, saying, "We have heard him speak blasphemous words against Moses and God." And they stirred up the people and the elders and scribes caught him and set him before the Council and employed false witnesses against him. They said, "We have heard him say that this Jesus of Nazareth shall destroy this place and shall change the customs that Moses delivered unto us." Those who sat in the Council, looking steadfastly on him, Stephen, saw his face as it was the face of an angel. Then the High Priest said, "Are these things so?"

After the priest had questioned Stephen about the accusations against him, Stephen spent an extended period of time reflecting on the history of Israel. Following his extended presentation, he finally said to them, "Ye stiff-necked and uncircumcised in heart and ears, ye do always resist the Holy Spirit; as your father did, so do ye." The record is that they were cut to the heart, and they gnashed on Stephen with their teeth. He looked steadfastly to Heaven; he saw the Son of God sitting on the right hand of the Father; they stoned Stephen...the deacon...but he prayed for them.

#5

"EXPERIENCE ON THE HIGHWAY"
(Acts 9:10-16)

"And there was a certain disciple at Damascus, named Ananias; and to him said the Lord in a vision, **Ananias.** And he said, Behold, I am here, Lord. **(11)** And the Lord said unto him, Arise, and go into the street which is called Straight, and inquire in the house of Judas for one called Saul of Tarsus; for, behold, he prayeth, **(12)** And hath seen in a vision, a man, named Ananias, coming in and putting his hand on him, that he might receive his sight. **(13)** Then Ananias, answered, Lord, I have heard by many of this man, how much evil he hath done to the saints at Jerusalem; **(14)** And here he hath authority from the chief priests to bind all that call on thy name. **(15)** But the Lord said unto him, Go thy way; for he is a chosen vessel unto me, to bear my name before the Gentiles, and kings, and the children of Israel; **(16)** For I will show him how great things he must suffer for my name's sake."

"And as he thus spoke for himself, Festus said with a loud voice, Paul, thou art beside thyself; much learning doth make thee mad. **(25)** But he said, I am not mad, most noble Festus, but speak forth the words of truth and soberness. **(26)** For the king knoweth of these things, before whom also I speak freely; for I am persuaded that none of these things are hidden from him; for this thing was not done in a corner" (**<u>Acts 26:24-26</u>**).

Read carefully the background, etc. It has been said that the most impressive things about an event is where it **happened;** when it **happened;** to whom it **happened;** and the **cause for which it happened!** It is not less true concerning the events that claim our attention here.

In our scripture references cited here, the Apostle Paul is relating to King Agrippa one of the most significant experiences of his life; that is, Paul's life! This unusual experience gripped Paul as he and a posse of deputies journeyed to Damascus. Their primary purpose for making this unusual visit was to arrest one of Christ's preachers and, thereby, destroying the movement of a religion that had been inspired by the **life/death/resurrection/and ascension of Jesus Christ.** This cadre of travelers had written permission from the High Priest to arrest anyone they discovered calling on the name of Jesus. Their purpose for this action was to curtail the spread of Christianity.

I need to remind us at this juncture that there was an old preacher in a little town called Damascus; a city of Asia, some **133** miles northeast of Jerusalem, who had a divine mission to carry out. This preacher, Brother **Ananias,** had begun an evangelistic move-ment that had its center in the personality of the risen Christ. This preacher's movement was stirring the country to such an extent that people were joining the cause in great numbers. Saul, being an officer of the law, attached himself to the Temple Court for the purpose of expanding the cause of Judaism. His purpose was to break up the movement and to put an end to the preacher's practice of highlighting the evangelistic influence of the risen Christ. His court order spelled out in detail that he was empowered to proceed to Damascus, and to arrest anyone, men or women, that were found guilty of calling on the name of Jesus. Such violators were to be brought back to Jerusalem and confined in the common jail until they were brought to trial. But on his way to Damascus to make the arrest, Saul himself was arrested by the Holy Spirit; the high sheriff of the Universe! He was arrested, sentenced, and assigned to a task of hard labor on the rock pile of Christian service...for the rest of his natural life.

It is to be noted that the words of our text are some of the divine reflexes of this great apostle. As he stands before Agrippa, defending himself against the many false charges by his fellow countrymen, he stood fast on his conviction. Some months earlier, something happened to Paul that changed his plans and outlook on life. This change in his life was so disturbing, that when he began to recite the incident before Festus, Festus cried out with a loud voice, "Paul, thou art beside thyself: much learning doth make the mad" (**Acts 26:24**).

The thing that disturbed Agrippa and his council was the sudden change in the attitude and outlook of the man who had sought so desperately to keep the fires of Judaism burning in their hearts. Because of his changed attitude, he had been arrested and was in jail at Caesarea, awaiting the outcome of the trial.

And it is to be realized and understood that in all great, spiritual movements, God's hand can be seen directing the affairs of all things and pulling the heartstrings of the conditions of times. In this connection, I urge you to study carefully the **24th, 25th, & 26th** chapters of the Acts of the Apostles. God's plan is clearly demonstrated and understood. Here, we see Paul standing before Agrippa, relating the history of the charges that were falsely lodged against him by his countrymen. As he stands there, Festus accuses him of being "beside himself," a victim of "egotism." He also accuses him of being over-learned and over-educated! He accuses him of knowing so much about things that he had become unbalanced and irrational to the extent that he had become insane! What an accusation!

The record is that with a loud voice, Festus cried out, "Paul, thou art beside thyself; you have too much sense. Much learning has made you mad" **(Acts 26:24)**. But at this point, Paul, wrapped in the security of the Holy Spirit, responded: "I am not mad, most Noble Festus, but I am swayed by the Great flow of truth within me." Festus had mis-judged Paul in calculating his ability and power of speech. Because power is not always eloquence, but eloquence is always powerful! The thing that happened to this great apostle had made him both eloquent and powerful. So he was able to say, "I am not mad, most Noble Festus, but speak forth the words of truth and soberness." For this thing was not done in a corner" **(Acts 26:25 & 26)**.

We note that in this conversation, Paul was referring to his conversion, when he was overpowered by the Holy Spirit and fell to the ground on that Damascus highway, as he journeyed toward the city of Damascus. Paul said that, "This thing was not done in a corner." One of the most amazing things about any conversion is that it happens; and when it does, it will be made known, and where it happened will be revealed also. And to whom it happens, whether man or woman, they will proclaim it unto the world. You cannot hide the fact of true conversion, the experience of being born again. *(My personal experience; Summer of 1932; Mt. Zion BC, Billingsley, Alabama; Monday night...Mother Laura & Ann Mall)*. What an experience; what an experience!

And so my dear listeners, even though the apostle was addressing the king, he was not ashamed to recall those unforgettable experiences on the "highway." He was not ashamed, nor afraid, to proclaim that this thing was not done in a corner. This thing, which you say has made me mad; this thing which you say has put arrogance in me; this thing which has caused such a radical change in me and the outlook of my life; I must confess to you that this thing was not done in a corner! It happened on the highway! This thing that makes the conversion of Paul such an overwhelming event is how he describes the place of its happening.

Permit me to remind you that highways are noted for many different occurrences. The pages of history are crowded with the acts of the highway. But never before has been said anything about a conversion on the highway. But in our text, Paul rises and tells the king, "It happened on the highway!" We need to remind ourselves that the greatest, most important event that can happen in life, to an individual, is his conversion or new birth! And whenever it occurs, it's a highway experience because the converted will surely bring it to the front. So Paul says to Agrippa, "It happened on the highway." Praise the Lord!

Friends, as I conclude this message, permit me to remind you again that everywhere that Paul went after that eventful day; to preach the glorious gospel of Jesus Christ, he reminded his listeners of his "Highway" experience. That voice that spoke to him and that light that was splashed in his face, and that fall to the ground, out yonder on the Damascus road, was an unforgettable experience in the life of Paul. So when he was brought before the king, in chains, in order to speak in his own defense, he thought of the "Highway" experience. Permit me now to recapture this whole story, so as to get a full understanding of Paul's experience. Please journey with me, as we begin our walk with Paul. Remember, "It Happened On The Highway."

Remember, we're dealing with "An Experience On The Highway." The Bible declares in **Acts 9:3-16,** these infallible words: **(3)** "And as he journeyed, he came near Damascus, and suddenly there shined round about him a light from heaven; **(4)** And he fell to the earth, and heard a voice saying unto him, **Saul, Saul, why persecutest thou me? (5)** And he said, Who art thou, Lord? And the Lord said, **I am Jesus, whom thou persecutest; it is hard for thee to kick against the pricks (goads). (6)** And he (Paul) trembling and astonished, said, Lord, what wilt thou have me to do? And the Lord said unto him, **Arise, and go into the city, and it shall be told thee what thou <u>must</u> do. (7)** And the men who journeyed with him stood speechless, hearing a voice, but seeing no man. **(8)** And Saul arose from the earth, and when his eyes were opened, he saw no man; but they led him by the hand, and brought him into Damascus. **(9)** And he was three days without sight, and neither did eat nor drink. (Remember, this is "<u>Experience On The Highway</u>"). **(10)** And there was a certain disciple at Damascus, named Ananias; and to him said the Lord in a vision, **<u>Ananias.</u>** And he said, Behold, I am here, Lord. **(11)** And the Lord said unto him, **Arise, and go into the street which is called Straight, and inquire in the house of Judas for one called Saul of Tarsus; for, behold, he prayeth, (12) And hath seen in a vision a man, named Ananias, coming in and putting his hand on him, that he might receive his sight.** **(13)** Then Ananias answered, Lord, I have heard by many of this man, how much evil he hath done to thy saints at Jerusalem; **(14)** And here he hath authority from the chief priests to bind all that call on thy name. **(15)** But the Lord said unto him, **Go thy way; for he is a chosen vessel unto me, to bear my name before the Gentiles, and kings, and the children of Israel; (16) For I will show him how great things he must suffer for my name's sake."**

Oh dear friends, do you recall when it happened to you? Do you recall the time and place when it happened? Do you recall the circumstances around its happening? It may not have been on the highway; it may not have been in the house of worship; it may not have been in your earthly dwelling place, but you should remember! You should remember! You should remember! Oh, how well do I remember.

#6

"HE THINKS OF ME"
(Psalm 40:1-3, 16,17)

"I waited patiently for the LORD, and he inclined unto me, and heard my cry. He brought me up also out of an horrible pit, out of the miry clay, and set my feet upon a rock, and established my goings. And he hath put a new song in my mouth, even praise unto our God; many shall see it, and fear, and shall trust in the LORD. Let all those who seek thee rejoice and be glad in thee; let such as love thy salvation say continually, The LORD be magnified. But I am poor and needy; yet the Lord thinketh upon me. Thou art my help and my deliverer; make no tarrying, O my God."

Philippians 4:19. "But my God shall supply all your need according to His riches in glory by Christ Jesus."

1 Peter 5:7. "Casting all your cares upon him; for he careth for you."

My brothers and my sisters, I sincerely believe that we can all agree that these scriptural references that I have used suggest that God is concerned about the welfare of all of His creatures. As I have been reflecting on these passages, I concluded that not only does God think of us, but He also cares for us.

It is sweet to be remembered, but it is bitter to be forgotten. I believe that many of the sorrows and woes of this life are due to a famishing heart; a heart that sighs, a heart that cries and dies for the want of human love, sympathy, appreciation and understanding.

That great poet, **William Shakespeare,** once declared that "Men are men; the best forget." But that renowned Psalmist, David, stated, "I am poor and needy, yet the Lord thinketh upon me." It can be stated with certainty that "men are men and they do forget; but God is God, and He never forgets."

To that drooping spirit, our text words are filled with tonic for the fainting heart. To me, our text words soothe like the fresh air from the mountain peak. Look at our text words. To me, they cheer like the sunbeam that pierces the fog in the mid-night hour. They soothe like the strains of an evening song. They comfort like a voice from among the stars. For it says, "I am poor and needy; yet, the LORD thinketh upon me."

Permit me now to explore more fully with you the meaning of the text, at least to me. Its sweetness is emphasized when we remember the many things about which our God must think. Try to grasp the greatness of this Universe; and the perpetual care of its august Maker and Ruler. How shall we conceive the idea of one world, not to mention countless worlds? Let us begin with the earth; the planet upon which we live. It is the only planet with which mankind shares any degree of compatibility. Some theologians and astrologers have calculated that earth's diameter is nearly 8,000 miles; its velocity is **nineteen miles** per second and its annual journey is **560 million** miles through space.

Try to imagine, if you will, this mass called earth, and seek to describe it by using these imposing figures. Climb some mountain peak and permit your eyes to scan the horizon and your imagination to soar and wander. Take a ship and travel 1,000 miles each day. Or take some fleeting train and spend a lifetime going from kingdom to kingdom, or from country to country. Pause occasionally and look upon some island flashing like an emerald upon the bosom of a purple sea. Spend an hour or two talking about the lands you've visited, or the cathedral splendors that have charmed you; the wild waste of desert that has impressed and oppressed you; the mountains which have awed you; the streams which have fascinated you; the flowers with their color and fragrance; the birds with their plumage and songs; the beasts of the fields; the fish of the sea, the minerals of the earth, the jewels that display their dazzling rays, and the human beings of all sorts, hues, and nationalities. Spend all your years in continual going until your voice is hushed in death, and you will not have seen one thousandth part of this vast Universe; and will not so much as begin to penetrate toward its far-off center! And yet, He who thinks of you and me created and sustains this great sphere.

Beginning at the sun as a station, someone has calculated that it would take 108 years for an express train, traveling at thirty-five-and-one-half miles per hour to reach the planet Mercury. It would take that train; traveling at the same speed, **204 years** to reach the planet Venus. It would take 426 years to reach Mars; 1,450 years to reach Jupiter; and 8,325 years to arrive at Neptune, the farthest point in the our solar system. But were we to send our train to the planet Sirius, the nearest fixed star, without stopping, it would take 60,000 years to reach that starry depot! There are many other, amazing statistics that scientists have calculated about the systems of the universe. But think about it! With all these worlds and systems of worlds and epic-systems of worlds, God is everywhere and the worlds must be kept in balance by Him. But, remember, David has declared that He thinketh of me.

On the horizon, I am but a pauper, but He thinks of me. Thank God I am not lost in the universal vastness of things, nor wedged in the quagmire of nothingness; He thinks of me! This wonderful universe; with all of its complexities, does not displace me in the mind and heart of my God. He thinks of me! He gave His Son to be my Savior; He knows all the hairs of my head; He calls them by name. He is familiar with all my sorrows; and He is not unmindful of poverty and needs. The Universe is not so massive, nor important, that He overlooks this humble creature. **He Thinks Of Me.**

Friends, the sweetness of this text are further enhanced when we remember the multitude of things about which God must think. Think of the countless units in God's Universe. Up, where stands the burning throne of God on the rim of glory, are innumerable angels that shine like lights; **seraphim,** who veil their faces with flamed-scorched wings and cry , "Holy, Holy, Holy; Lord God Almighty; the **cherubim,** whose songs drip with celestial praise; innumerable ranks, and principalities, and power; might and dominions of the heavenly host; all fit subjects to attract the thought and delight of God. But in the midst of all of these, "He Thinks Of Me." Out, above, beyond, around, and beneath the throne of God, swimming in the blue amplitudes of space, are countless suns and moons and stars and comets and nebulae; a blazing host which none but He can even count. **"Yet He Thinks Of Me."**

Down here on earth are men of various types and temperaments that are embellished with an infinite variety of fauna and flora, minerals and motes, which no human calculus can express numerically. We cannot number the items in God's Universe, and if we attempted to do so we would fail miserably.

But God knows them and must think of them. Every star in the universe must be lighted and fixed in its golden socket. Every angel must be sent on his mission of light. Every man must be placed in his plan, so as to do no violence to his free agency. Every devil and demon must be held in check. The young lion must be given his food. The throat of every linnet must be kept in tune. The cheek of every lily must be painted. Every opal must be made to flash as though dipped in red wine. Every robin's breast must be colored, and every bird must have its song and season to sing. From the tallest archangel which treads the mosaic of yonder sky to the humblest lichen on the swampy log; everything must be held in perpetual remembrance by Him who sits upon the flaming circle of the heaven and looks on the nations as grasshoppers. Yet, the Lord thinks upon me! He helps me. He sympathizes with me. He loves me. He understands me. He provides for me. I am not sunk in the multitudes and forgotten. I am not lost in the many. I am never overlooked, because He has so many things to consider. No, no, He thinks of me!

Friends, we need to remind ourselves that the beauty of this text is enhanced when we consider the complexity of the things which our God has to consider. The starry systems of the universe must be contained. The wild comets, dashing through space, must be held in check. Angels and archangels and angelic organizations stand before His throne for guidance. Kings and nations and individuals must be moved at His command. In this universe alone there are innumerable forces that call for His attention. Mechanical forces, chemical forces, electrical forces, atmospheric forces, psychological forces, angelic forces, and even satanic forces must act at His command. Forces above within forces; forces under forces; forces against forces; all must be sustained, controlled and utilized. Oh, what a complexity of things that our God must think about. **Yet, He thinketh of me!**

Friends, the wonderfulness of this text is clearly brought out if we pause to consider the greatness and glory of God, the Being who always has us in His thoughts, upon His mind, and in His heart! He keeps us as the apple of His eye. As those who remember us rise in scales of being, character and position, they soon forget us. But He remembers us always.

Finally, the wonderfulness of this text is enhanced when I consider myself as the object of God's incomparable thoughtfulness.

Yes, I may be poor and needy and in my own power, I possess nothing with which to make my own life comfortable. I am just a "bundle" of wants, with no means of supplying them without God's intervention. Without God, I am just a beggar and a pauper. I have nothing, and without God, I am nothing! When God takes me upon His hands, He simply takes a whining and complaining creature. More often than not, He takes an individual who continually forgets the hand that feeds him and the heart that warms him. **Yet, HE thinks of me.**

Yes, the Universe may be great, its items may be many, its affairs may be complex. God may be great and He is great. I may be poor and needy, destitute and worthless. Yet, the Lord thinks of me. Men may misunderstand me, but He knows my whole story. Men may forget me, but He remembers me. Men may despise me, but He loves me. He is never too busy to come and see about me. **<u>He Thinks Of Me.</u>**

#7

"ROBBERS IN THE CHURCH"
(Malachi 3:7-10)
Tithing

Four hundred fifty years before the birth of Christ, the Prophet Malachi accused Israel of a serious infraction of God's Law. Listen to his words in **Malachi 3:7-l0:** "Even from the days of your fathers ye are gone away from mine ordinances, and have not kept them. Return unto me, and I will return unto you, saith the LORD of host. But ye said, in what way shall we return. Will a man rob God? Yet ye have robbed me. But ye say, How have we robbed thee? **In tithes an offerings.** Ye are cursed with a curse; for ye have robbed me, even this whole nation. Bring all the tithes into the storehouse, that there may be meat (food) in mine house, and prove (test) me now herewith, saith the LORD of hosts, if I will not open for you the windows of heaven, and pour out for you a blessing, that there shall not be room enough to receive it."

Here, I want to read verses 11 and 12 to indicate what blessings God has reserved for those who will obey His Word. Malachi states in these two verses: "(ll) And I will rebuke the devourer for your sakes, and he shall not destroy the fruits of your ground; neither shall your vine cast its fruit before the time in the field, saith the LORD of hosts. (l2) And all nations shall call you blessed; for ye shall be a delightsome land, saith the LORD of hosts."

258

Note what Jesus said when He announced seven woes upon the Pharisees. He said in **Matthew 23:23,** *"Woe unto you, scribes and Pharisees, hypocrites! For ye pay tithes of mint and anise and cumin, and have omitted the weightier matters of the law,* **justice, mercy,** *and* **faith;** *these ought ye to have done, and not leave the other undone."*

Before continuing this message, I would ask this simple question: What type and kind of giving did God require of Israel and what does He require of us? As it relates to Israel, I suggest that you carefully read **Exodus 35:1-35,** with focus on **Exodus 35:22.** The record is that "Both men and women came; all whose hearts were willing. Some brought to the LORD their offerings of gold; medallions; earrings; rings from their fingers, and necklaces. They presented gold objects of every kind to the LORD." It is to be noted that God is pleased when we give generously. Often times we will limit our giving to 10 percent, but the Bible says we should give from the heart all that we are able. **2 Corinthians 8:12 & 2 Corinthians 9:6-7, also Deuteronomy 14:22-23,** give us a clear indication of how we should give to support the Word of the Lord.

Tithing is a clear way to demonstrate our priorities. The Bible makes it unmistakably clear that tithing indicates that we put God first in our lives. What we do first with our money reveals what we value most. I suggest to us that our first giving should always be God. Giving the first part of our paycheck to God immediately focuses our attention on Him.

I must admit that the subject chosen for this message, **"<u>Robbers</u> <u>In The Church,</u>"** is a penetrating and, perhaps, an uncomfortable one! When one thinks of the word **"Robber"** or **"Robbery,"** he immediately thinks of an act that is being performed with the knowledge of the victim. How true this is with those who do not comply with the teaching of God's Word. To be sure, God is knowledgeable that He is being robbed by His creatures.

How often does one hear the phrase from avowed Christians in the church who will state emphatically that tithing was an Old Testament requirement? But listen to what Jesus said to those Pharisees, hypocrites! He said, "For ye pay tithes of mint and anise and cumin, and have omitted the weightier matter of the law, justice, mercy, and faith; these ought ye to have done, and not to leave the other undone." Note this Good News translation of **Matthew 23:23:** "How terrible of you, teachers of the law and Pharisees! You hypocrites! You give God one tenth even of the seasoning herbs, such as mint, dill, and cumin, but you neglect to obey the really important teaching of the Law, such as justice and mercy and honesty. These you should practice, without neglecting the others – tithing."

According to the record, Jesus received tithes. Jesus practiced tithing. He commended it in others. And we must remember that God has always had a place for His tithe to be used. In the Old Testament, the tithe was ready and kept in the storehouse at all times. God said through His prophet, "Bring ye all the tithes into the storehouse." It is to be noted that if a person wanted to keep some of his flock, or herd, or whatever it was, he was to add a fifth part (interest, if you will) to the amount that was brought. In Hebrews 7:8, we understand that Jesus is the one who receives our tithes. He says here, "And here (in this life) men that die receive tithes; but there he receiveth them, of whom it is witnessed that he liveth." Speaking of Jesus!

In that seventh chapter of Hebrews, we read that **Melchizedek** was the first one ever to receive the tithes. This was long before the law had been enunciated. It was during the time of the existence of Abraham upon the earth. Melchizedek was King of Righteousness, the King of Salem; i.e., the King of Peace, "without father, without mother, without descent, had he neither beginning of days nor end of life; but made like unto the Son of God; abideth a priest continually." Praise the Lord. Melchizedek was a type of Jesus and he was the first one to receive tithes.

My brothers and my sisters, as I hasten on here, I need to emphasize Jesus' position on tithing. In His teaching, He seems to say to us that tithing alone is not sufficient. While Jesus practiced tithing, and commended it, and while it is He who receives it, He says that tithing alone is insufficient. That is what He said to the Pharisees. Tithing of money is no substitute for spirituality and morality. He said, "You have been paying your tithes. You have been putting ten percent into the treasury, but you have been neglecting the spiritual things, righteousness, mercy, morality." Tithing is no substitute for immortal virtues. You cannot buy your way. Tithing is insufficient in itself.

Jesus also indicates that the simple matter of keeping the letter of the law and giving a tithe is not sufficient. It should be a spiritual experience, above all else. It should be an experience that is grown out of love for Christ and love for the church and love for a lost world. My brothers and my sisters, when we bring our tithe and lay it upon the altar, it is part of ourselves, money that we earn. It is our time. It is our energy. It is our ability. It is a spiritual gift. Jesus also taught that the tithe is the minimum. It is not always enough. It is not always sufficient. When Jesus sat over against the treasury, He saw several who put in their gifts, but the one He commended was a dear, destitute sister, perhaps a widow, who put in just two pennies. He commended her because she gave more than all the rest had given. One thing the New Testament teaches above everything else in this matter of giving is the importance of the proportion.

As an individual is able, God provides the opportunity for him or her to give above and beyond the tithe. This is for his or her blessing and his or her good. My brothers and my sisters, I know of no better way to say it than in the words of Jesus Himself that somehow were not found in the gospel, but Dr. Luke included these words in the book of Acts. He said in **Acts 20:35,** *"It is more blessed to give than to receive."*

And finally, my brothers and my sisters, I do not want us to get lost in the letter of the law. I want, above all else, that we would get lost in Jesus, in our love for Christ that would lead us to lay our all upon the altar for Him. As I speak to us today, it is my prayer that all of us will permit the tithe to be but the beginning, and keep on until we've given our all for Him. My friends, think of those that have gone out on some of our foreign mission fields, giving their entire lives for the cause of Christ. What do you think a tithe is in comparison to the sacrifice that they have made? When we think of Jesus Christ dying on the cross for our sins, paying the supreme price, the ultimate, for our redemption, what do you think a tithe is, your tithe, my tithe, in comparison to the price that Christ paid for our salvation? Look at Jesus hanging on the cross and crying out, "My God, my God, why hast thou forsaken me?" and then look at your tithe. Oh, my dearly beloved, lay your all on the altar for Jesus.

My brothers and my sisters, as we gather on this first Lord's day of this third month of this year 2003, may we all take a personal inventory of our lives and determine how we stand with God insofar as our obedience to His word is concerned. Look at our commitment, not only in terms of our tithe, but our Christian commitment to the cause of Christ. I admonish you today that if you have never seriously considered tithing; if you've been procrastinating about this important decision, I urge you to make that decision today. Remember, the tithe is holy and the tithe belongs to God. God spoke through His prophet, Malachi in these words, "You've robbed me; you are cursed with a curse." If you did not come prepared to tithe today, remember when you come next Sunday, come with your tithe to present to the Lord.

#8

"SHOW ME GOD"

"Let not your heart be troubled; ye believe in God, believe also in me. In my Father's house are many mansions; if it were not so, I would have told you. I go to prepare a place for you. And if I go and prepare a place for you, I will come again, and receive you unto myself, that where I am, there ye may be also. And where I go ye know, and the way ye know. Thomas saith unto him, Lord, we know not where thou goest; and how can we know the way? Jesus saith unto him, I am the **way,** the **truth,** and the **life,** no man cometh unto the Father, but by me. If ye had known me, ye should have known my Father also; and from henceforth ye know him, and have seen him. Philip saith unto him, Lord, show us the Father, and it sufficieth us." **(John 14:1-8)**

The verses that I've shared with you contain a conversation that takes place between Jesus, Thomas and Philip, in the Passover chambers in Jerusalem, as Jesus relates and foretells His departure and return. Specifically, our text words were born out of a discussion between Jesus and Thomas. Thomas had posed this question, **John 14:5,** "Lord, we know not where you are going, and how can we know the way?" Jesus had spoken about the many mansions in His Father's house, and His soon departure for that house. Thomas wanted to know how to get there! Jesus replied, "I am the way, the truth, and the life; no man cometh unto the Father, but by me" And then He said to Thomas; who had posed the question as to how he might get there: If I were to use today's vernacular words, I would say, "Thomas, where have you been?" Listen, "If ye had known me, ye should have known my Father also, and henceforth ye know him, and have seen Him" **(John 14:7).**

Pause with me for a moment, as we reflect on the text words. We begin by analyzing the position of the disciples, in a contemporary form. For example, a **Skeptic,** an **Agnostic,** or an **Atheist** may have been justified in making the request that Philip made, but Philip should have not made the request to see the Father; for the very work of Jesus had identified His relationship with the Father and thoroughly testified of the Lordship of Jesus. You see, Philip was a constant companion of Jesus. Philip was there when Jesus turned water into wine at the marriage in Cana **(John 2:6-12).** Philip was there when Jesus fed the **5,000** at the Sea of Tiberia with five barley loaves and two fishes **(John 6:1-3).** Philip was there when Jesus raised Lazarus from the dead in Bethany **(John 11:43).** Yes, Philip was there when Jesus calmed the sea **(Mark 4:35-4l).** Philip was an eyewitness to these miracles and should have known that Jesus was the very God!

Take a careful look at the story; to whom were Thomas and Philip speaking? A good question, to be sure. They were speaking to: Jesus, the lowly Nazarene; my Mighty God; my Prince of Peace. They were speaking to Jesus, my rock in a weary land and my shelter in the time of storm. They were speaking to Jesus, my bread in a starving land and my water when I'm thirsty. Oh, yes He was. They were speaking to Jesus, who gave up dignity for shame, honor for dishonor, and riches to become poor. One who got out of a chariot in glory and got on a bare-backed donkey and rode triumphantly into Jerusalem. One who left the gold-paved streets of yonder's heaven, to walk the rough and rocky hills of Judah, and the deserts of Galilee. They were speaking with Jesus. Like a young roe came leaping from the highest heights of heaven to the lowest depths of hell, Jesus came. Yes, He came unto His own, but they received Him not **(John 1:11).** This Jesus went about doing good, healing the sick, cleansing leprosy, giving sight to the blind, and raising the dead, but He was rejected! My brothers and my sisters, this Jesus took the Roman cross, long a symbol of defeat, and transformed it into a key that would unlock the doors of hell and lead paradise from these lower mundane shores to the third heaven; heavens of heaven. This was the Christ to whom Philip spoke.

Show Me God. I need to emphasize again that the sole purpose for Christ's coming into the world was to reveal His Father and to redeem man from the curse of sin. All He said and all that He did were simply by products of His main purpose for coming: to reveal God to man and to save man from his sins! Men of all ages have longed to see God. Moses on Mt. Sinai asked for a face-to-face conference with God. He was denied the privilege! There have been interpretations and re-interpretations of just who He is and what He's like. A further examination of this text, and surrounding textual references, reveal a need to talk from four general headings:

(1) *"The mis-conception of Jesus."* (2) *"When God is demonstrated"* (3) *"We can go to the wrong place to see God, and (4) "When we need to see God."*

The Misconception Of God: We recall now that for three years, the disciples had left all of their families and possessions to follow Jesus. Yes, they had left their boats and nets on the seashore of Galilee. They had forsaken family and friends, and the religion of Judaism to follow Jesus. But here Jesus announces He is going back to the Father; they can't follow Him now, so they are concerned. "Who will care for us?" Well, Jesus says to them, "I'm going to leave you in the hands of my Father." Philip, at this point, and no doubt speaking for the entire group of disciples, makes this sincere request: "Lord, show us the Father and that sufficeth us." In other words, Philip seems to say here, "Jesus, we've known You and have been with You for almost two years; we know You're able; we've tried You; we can trust You; we've left all to follow You. And now You're going to leave us with the Father, of whom we know little or nothing. We want to know Him; we've never seen Him." Here, Jesus speaks to Philip: "Have I been so long time with you, and yet thou hast not known me, Philip?" **(John 14:9).** "He that hath seen me hath seen the Father; and how saith thou then, show us the father?" Here, Jesus called Philip by name, an indication of the seriousness of the matter.

We observe here that the misconception of God on this occasion is so serious. I hear Jesus say, "I have been with you for all this time; seeking to show you God, but you have not perceived Him! My Father and I are one and when you see Me you see My Father. I came to show God to a dying world! Do you now remember, Philip, that I attended the wedding feast at Cana of Galilee; all of the wine was consumed; six water pots were filled to the brim with water and when I peered into the water pots, the water got a view of My face, blushed and turned into wine! Philip, you recall Me raising Jairus' daughter from the dead; you were at Bethany when I raised Lazarus from his four day's grave slumber; and yet, you ask to see God. Philip, all of these things you've witnessed; you've seen Me perform these miracles. Philip, what more do you expect from God? Philip, I AM GOD; you've been seeing the Father all along."

The world today wants to see God in the church. The world stands yonder in the valley, with outstretched hands and a feeble voice, looking to the church, that city on a hill, and crying, "<u>Show Me God.</u>" The world wants to see God in every Christian, and we should have no greater mission than to reveal Him to lost mankind.

When God Is Demonstrated: My brothers and my sisters, when, through our lives and our action, God is demonstrated in our **homes,** in our **churches,** and in our **individual lives,** God will get the glory that He rightfully deserves. Someone has stated so aptly that when God walks, strange things happen. Lions shake dew drops from their manes; panthers quit speaking and snakes uncoil themselves. When God walks, the tempestuous wind on the infested deep recognizes His voice and behaves accordingly.

When He speaks, the forked and zigzag lightening quits playing her limber game on the bosom of the blue ether; the waves stop fighting, the winds cease to blow, the white caps quit bursting on the bosom of the mighty deep; and the thunder goes back to bed, when God walks! When He walks, angels adore Him, the four and twenty elders cast down their glittering crowns and the four beasts say Amen. When God walks, creation trembles like a leaf on the tree; sinners scream with horror and devils howl with vexation of spirit; when God walks. OH! **"Show Me God"**

We Can Go To The Wrong Place Seeking God: Yes, many times, I'm afraid, we miss God by going to the wrong places looking for Him. If I were to ask Zacchaeus, the tax collector and citizen of Jericho, he would have this story: **(Luke 9:1-10)** You know the story! Zacchaeus, the tax collector and citizen of Jericho, heard that Jesus was passing through his region. Zacchaeus closed his shop one day, hung out his "Office Closed" and rushed out of his office to get a view of Jesus. The record is that he climbed a sycamore tree. (story) Jesus bade him come down! Permit me to remind us that a high and lofty place may not be the place to meet Jesus. Jesus, that man whom I love so well, please tell me where He dwells? The answer could very well be: "Go down and search among the poor; you'll find Him there."

When We See God; When We Need God: In this life, we need to have the right relationship with God. We need to know that God is with us in this world, through His Son Jesus the Christ. Like

Daniel in the lion's den; like Shadrach, Meshach, and Abednego in the fiery furnace; like the Apostle Paul who was pestered with thorns in his flesh, we need to know that God's grace is sufficient.

My brothers and my sisters, when we come face to face with death, we need to see God. The thief on that rugged cross got his only experience of God while facing death. In the throes of death, I hear him pray, "Lord, remember me when thou cometh into thy Kingdom" **(Luke 23:42).**

In my imagination, *I heard Jesus speak to death and said, here's a man that wants to see God. I want you to wait long enough for me to show him God. Death said, no Jesus, I can't wait! Usually, when men get to the point where you are, they get in a hurry; yet, you want me to wait. When Abraham got here he wanted to get it all over; he dashed across the foamy Jordan, for he looked for a city that had foundations whose builder and maker is God. Jesus said to death, I said wait! I gave you the right to ride; I put you on your pale horse and put that sword in your sheath; I say wait! Death apologized to Jesus and waited.* Jesus said to the thief, "Today, thou shalt be with me in paradise" **(Luke 23:43).**

Friends, when we meet the Lord in the air, we will need a vision of God. I want to see Him for myself someday. What about you? In my mind, I see that hosts of heaven, making themselves acquainted with me. Peter, James, John, the disciples and prophets, will come and shake my hand. I'll say in response to their question, "Grace has brought me here and I'm glad to meet you. BUT SHOW ME

GOD! I want to see that Christ who cut loose stammering tongues and put a new song in my mouth: That man who stopped my feet from dancing; that man who stopped my tongue from lying. Show Me That Man." I see twelve pearly gates; I see the host who have washed their robes and made them white in the blood of the Lamb; those that came up out of great tribulation; those that have borne their burdens in the heat of the day. BUT SHOW ME GOD!

Friends, I'm not there yet, but until I get there, I'll be satisfied to see God in the budding of the trees at springtime; the falling of the leaves in autumn evening; the muttering thunder, and the flashing of lightening; the cry of that newborn babe. Early in the morning, I want Him to touch me with a fingertip of love, and say good morning, my good and faith servant; wake up. Show Me God!

#9

"WEEPING OVER THE CITY"
(Luke 19:40,41)

"And he answered and said unto them, *I tell you that, if these should hold their peace, the stones would immediately cry out.* And when he was come near, he beheld the city, and wept over it." (GNB-TEV) "Jesus answered, 'I tell you that if they keep quiet, the stones themselves will start shouting.' He came closer to the city, and when he saw it, he wept over it."

Weeping Over The City — As we observe this story, we quickly discover that Jesus and His disciples are now in Jerusalem. For Jesus and the inhabitants of Jerusalem and its surrounding regions, this was Passover. And as Jesus approached the close of His earthly ministry, we observe that it was only three years earlier that John the Baptist had introduced Him to the multitude at the Jordan River by saying to them, **"Behold the Lamb of God, which the sin of the world" (John 2:29).** But this is all behind now and this Galilean is entering Jerusalem for the last time.

His fame had spread quickly throughout the region. He was hailed as a great teacher, miracle worker, and lover of children. There were those who went so far as to call Him the Messiah. When and wherever He moved, He could not free Himself from the people, because of His popularity. But He is in Jerusalem now. Up to this point, He had guarded well the secret of His Messiahship. On the mountain of transfiguration, when the three disciples witnessed

His glory, Jesus cautioned them to tell no one until the proper time. Now the time had come. He would permit the people to acclaim Him King. The time had arrived for the fulfillment of Zechariah's prophecy that stated, "Rejoice greatly, O daughter of Zion; shout, O daughter of Jerusalem: behold, thy King cometh unto thee lowly, and riding upon an ass, and upon a colt, the foal of an ass" (**Zechariah 9:9**).

If you will, look at the city over which Jesus wept. The gentle spring rains had fallen. The countryside had begun to turn green. The various types of flowers had added their brightness to the meadow, as the pomegranate and honeysuckle filled the gentle air with their fragrance. It was a beautiful spring morning. Having completed breakfast with His disciples and their friends, Jesus departs Bethany for Jerusalem. We observe from the record that by the time they had reached Bethphage, the road was crowded with pilgrims who were making their annual visit to the Feast of the Passover. Preparation was necessary, as indicated in **Luke 19:29-34.** The record reveals that in the morning that Jesus entered Jerusalem triumphantly, He had previously sent two of His disciples to prepare for His entry. They found the colt tied as Jesus had informed them. Upon loosing the colt, the owner asked, "Why loose ye the colt?" They replied, "The Lord hath need of him." Quit willingly, the owner of the colt consented to release the colt for use by the Lord. What is the lesson here for us? We, too, should dedicate our possessions for the use of our Lord. (Praise His holy name)!

As Jesus seated Himself upon the colt, and began His visit into Jerusalem, there must have been some inquisitive minds that questioned, "Who is this?" The record is that the disciples and others replied, "It is He who cometh in the name of the Lord." The roadway into the city of Jerusalem was crowed; people were excited; children and parents joined in the cries of blessing. One may reason that this holiday crowd joined in shouting portions of tha

t **24th Psalm of David.** "Lift up your head heads, O ye gates; and be ye lift up, ye everlasting doors; and the King of glory shall come in" **(v.7).** Those that went on before may have shouted, "Who is this King of glory?" while those who followed replied, "The LORD strong and mighty, the LORD mighty in battle."

My brothers and my sisters, as we observe this little donkey jogging toward the Kidron Valley, those on the outskirts of the city now joined the accolade about the Master. The entire valley now rings with the cries of **"Hosanna."** This Palm Sunday caravan would seem likely to get out of hand! Some of the Pharisees requested Jesus to rebuke the shouting disciples, but Jesus replied that if they would hold their peace, **"the stones would immediately cry out."** Following this reply by Jesus, some of the Pharisees cried out, "Behold the world is gone after him" **(John 12:19).**

It seems now that everyone was in the holiday spirit. Everyone was in a festive mood. Everyone was happy. Everyone, that is, except Jesus! The record indicates that He was hurt! He was unhappy! What a contrast of emotions! Yes, the wild demonstration by this fickle multitude moved Jesus to weep! While the people shouted **"Hosanna,"** Jesus' heart was broken into passionate lamentations; as He cried out, "O Jerusalem, Jerusalem, thou that killed the prophets and stonest them which are sent unto thee, how often would I have gathered thy children together, even as a hen gathereth her chicken under her wings, and ye would not" (**Matthew 23:3**) Notice here the lost love, **Luke 19:41-44.** Permit me to read these verses now: **(41)** "And when he was come near, he beheld the city, and wept over it, (42) Saying, *If thou hadst known, even thou, at least in this thy day, the things which belong unto thy peace! But now they are hid from thine eyes.* (43) For the days shall come upon thee, that thine enemies shall cast a trench about thee, and compass thee round, and keep thee in on every side, **(44)** And shall lay thee even with the ground, and thy children within thee; and they shall not leave in thee one stone upon another; because thou knewest not the time of thy visitation."

My brothers and my sisters, what we hear in these words is the agony of the Savior over a lost city. The phrase "how often" is a sorrowful summing up of the most tender story ever told! Never had a people been so loved as the children of Israel. They had been called out of strange places, sheltered in Egypt, delivered from bondage, and given a land flowing with milk and honey. God had done all this for them so that they in turn might bless all the nations of the earth. God's love for them is reflected in the parable of the lost sheep, the lost coin, and the lost son (Luke Chapter 15). "How often" was a love story that began with Father Abraham **eighteen centuries** earlier! But now their day of grace was about over and they still refused God's call for love. Jesus sorrowfully said, "And ye would not." The **Lost Opportunity (Luke 19:42**) "If thou hadst known, even thou, at least in this thy day, the things which belong unto thy peace! But now they are hid from thine eyes." The "IF" speaks of an opportunity offered and refused and lost forever! Israel had her time of salvation. You have yours and I have mine; and it is today! Israel had it when God gave them Moses and the prophets; when King David stretched the kingdom from Dan to Beersheba; again when she returned from Babylon to rebuild, and now in the person of Jesus the Messiah. But they killed the prophets and stoned those that were sent to deliver them. And now they would soon crucify the Son of God Himself.

Jesus, our Christ, wept that day for what Israel may have become had she remained true to her calling. But Israel missed her chance; she lost her opportunity. This is the sad story of too many lives! God has a purpose for our lives. He has a purpose for my life. He has a purpose for your life! He wills only the best for us, but we must be obedient to His calling. Some of you, perhaps on this Psalm Sunday, 2013, need to say "yes" to God's will for your lives. Do not permit this opportunity to be lost. For, as Jesus said, these are the "things that belong to thy peace." God's will is the way of peace and happiness for you now and for eternity. We have seen how Psalm Sunday was a day of Triumph, a day of Tragedy, and now the day of Tribulation. In **Luke 19:43 & 44,** it is clearly spelled out. Listen again to the words of the Messiah. He said, "For the days shall come upon thee, that thine enemies shall cast a trench about thee, and compass thee round, and keep thee in on every side, And shall lay thee even with the ground, and thy children within thee; and they shall not leave in thee one stone upon another; because thou knewest not the time of my visitation." *The Day of Tribulation.* This prophecy was fulfilled in A.D. 70 when Titus and his Roman army captured Jerusalem.

Here we are on this Psalm Sunday, 2013, and God is speaking to our hearts. Do not permit His weeping to be in vain, as it was for Israel. He came; yes He came, to seek and to save that which was lost. Will you accept Him today, if you have not previously accepted Him?

"If you hold your peace, the stones will cry out!" Do you want the stones to cry out for you? For me, No! No! No! He's been too good for me! When I was on my way to a devil's hell, one Monday evening I heard His voice speak to me, and I accepted His invitation. He's Mine! He's Mine! He's Mine!

#10

"WHEAT AND TARES"

Matthew 13:24-30

"Another parable put He forth unto them, saying, The kingdom of heaven is likened unto a man who sowed good seed in this field; But, while men slept, his enemy came and sowed tares among the wheat, and went his way. But when the blade was sprung up, and brought forth fruit, then appeared the fares also. So the servant of the householder came and said unto him, Sir, didst not thou sow good seed in thy field? From where, then hath it tares? He said unto them, An enemy hath done this. The servant said unto him, Wilt thou, then that we go and gather them up? But he said, Nay; lest while ye gather up the tares, ye root up also the wheat with them. Let both grow together until the harvest; and in the time of harvest I will say to the reapers, Gather together first the tares, and bind them in bundles to burn them, but gather the wheat into my barn"

(King James Translation)

Jesus then told them this story: The kingdom of heaven is like what happened when a farmer scattered good seed in a field. But while everyone was sleeping, an enemy came and scattered week seed in the field and then left. When the plants came up and began to ripen, the farmer's servants could see the weeds. The servants came and asked, "Sir, didn't you scatter good seed in your field? Where did these weeds come from?" "An enemy did this," he replied. His servants then asked, "Do you want us to go out and pull up the weeds?" "No!" he answered. "You might also pull up the wheat. Leave wheat alone until harvest time. Then I'll tell my workers to gather the weeds and tie them up and burn them. But I'll have them store the wheat in my barn." (**Contemporary English Version**)

This thirteenth chapter of the Gospel of Matthew contains fifty-eight verses and several distinct parables...all relating to the kingdom. In this chapter, we have the parable of the **Sower**; Parable of the **Tares among the Wheat;** Parable of the **Mustard Seed;** Parable of the **Leaven Bread;** Parable of the **Hidden Treasure; P**arable of the Goodly Pearls; and Parable of the Drag Net in the Sea. All of these parables are thought-provoking and worthy of in-depth study, for they speak of the Kingdom.

As we analyze these parables, we observe that only one of them deals specifically with the church, **"Tares Among Wheat!"** This parable relates chiefly to the condition of the church. In the natural sense, it is interesting to note the comparison: From wheat we get bread, and bread is the staple of the physical life. So why did Jesus use this parable? To warn His disciples of the danger of tares, and the danger of attempting to make the separation, based on man's limited knowledge! In the spiritual sense, as it related to the church: "Leave Them Alone!"

What are tares, as they relate to the church? It has been said that tares are those who outwardly profess Christian religion but inwardly reject it! And yet, they are intermingled with the Christians as the tares are intermingled with the wheat. The question: Was this is this by design? As Jesus spoke to His twelve disciples one day about the inconsistency of those who professed to be His true disciples, He said, "Have not I chosen you twelve, and one of you is a devil?" **(John 6:70)** Could the wheat and tares intermingling be by design, although an enemy sowed them? Is it true that we need to be temped and tested at times? How strong am I? How strong are you?

From this parable, we need to understand that there will always be good and bad in the church; right and wrong; saints and sinners! To be sure, it is difficult to distinguish one from the other, for it is not until the fruit comes that there is a noticeable difference. This is why Jesus warned His disciples in the Sermon on the Mount, "… By their fruits, ye shall know them." **(Matthew 7:20)**

The true meaning of this parable is, Jesus' teaching on the danger of professing without faith, or pretending to be what one knows he or she is not. In his Sermon on the Mount, Jesus said, "Not everyone that saith unto me, Lord, Lord, shall enter into the kingdom; but he that doeth the will of my father which is in heaven. Many will say to me in that day, Lord, Lord, have we not prophesied in thy name? And in thy name have cast out devils? And then will I profess unto them, I never knew you: depart from me, ye that work iniquity." **(Matthew 7:21-23).** My brothers and sisters, how carefully ought we to live.

Note, if you will, that good seeds were sown! That they were sown in good soil, that they were sown at the right season, for they sprung up. But note, also, that tares also sprung up! They were not sown, they were not blown there by the wind. Well, how did they get there? The answer is contained in verse #25. "While men slept, his enemy came and sowed tares among the wheat, and went his way." To be an effective witness for Christ, one must be alert. You see, the enemy is always lurking somewhere to entrap or beguile the believer. There is no time to pause along the wayside and pick flowers.

We, as believers, need to be alert and watchful. At night, when the evil one works... we need to be alert. The Bible declares that men love darkness, because their deeds are evil **(John 3:19).** Please note, my sisters and my brothers, it is as impossible for us to prevent hypocrites being in the church as it is for the husbandman, when he is asleep, to hinder an enemy from spoiling his field. And to be sure, sleep is a natural part of man's needs. Is there a dilemma? No! We must sow the best possible seed and leave the production to God! Be sure that the seeds that we are sowing are not corrupted by our own action. Praise the Lord!

The word here is that, "An enemy has done this!" He does not lay the blame on the servants; they could not help it, but had done only what was in their power to do. The ministers of Christ, and other faithful witnesses, shall not be judged as failures when they have faithfully done all that they could possibly do, and then find the bad with the good; the hypocrites with the sinners, all in the church family...the same church family! We, as believers, should take hope in the fact that there will come a day of reckoning and separation.

The text: "So the servants of the householder came and said unto him, 'Sir, didst not thou sow good seed in thy field? from whence then hath it tares?' He said unto them, 'An enemy hath done this. The servants said unto him, Wilt thou then that we go and gather them up?' But he said, 'Nay; lest while ye gather up the tares, ye root up also the wheat with them." **(Matthew 13-27-29)** The Good News Gospel gives this rendition: "The man's servant came to him and said, Sir, it was good seed you sowed in your field: where did the weeds come from? It was some enemy who did this, he answered. Do you want us to go and pull up the weeds? They asked him. No, he answered, because as you gather the weeds you might pull up some of the wheat along with them."

Permit me to serve notice on us today, tares are from the devil! They are not designed to help, but to hinder. And they are in the church, even as I speak. Leave them alone, it is not yet harvest time. These tares are not blown in by the wind; they are planted by the enemy. So it is with the church. Sometimes when the program of the church becomes stalled and ineffective, no good seeds have been sown. It is because tares may have been sown instead by the enemy. Let me serve notice on us again in that tares come in from unsuspected sources. Many times it seems almost impossible to move forward with the program of Christ's church. We pray, we sacrifice, we teach, we council, we give totally of ourselves and, at last, there seems to be failure. One begins to question everything; then the light of day will peek through.

May we consider, for just a few moments, some of the tares that are found in our churches today. Tares that will hinder, but cannot stop, the progress of Christ's church. And permit me to serve further notice on ourselves that if we are not careful and pray constantly and consistently, we may become one those who sow tares among the wheat. Note this, if you will. In the church, there are: tares of jealousy; tares of hate; tares of confusion; tares of strife; tares of doubt; tares of contention; tares of disobedience; tares of envy! No wonder the farmer proclaimed, "An enemy has done this!" These are the fruit of the enemy.

Yes, tares may be represented in a careless word; a slip of the tongue; malicious gossip; or countless other thoughtless deeds. But here is a note of encouragement. When you know that you are doing the very best that you can, try not to worry! You see, the enemy comes when you are asleep sometimes, and plant the seed of discord among the believers. There is nothing you can do about it but pray. But thanks be to God, He sees, He knows, He understands, and He will bring about the victory. Stay hard by your role.

Let us see Jesus. He went out of the house of the centurion in Capernaum, whose servant was sick; and sat by the seaside. Great multitudes were gathering together unto Him, so that He went into a ship, and the whole multitude stood on the shore... (Read Text)

BIBLE KNOWLEDGE

THE TWELVE TRIBES OF ISRAEL

Tribe #1: **DAN**: Dan was a son of Jacob. His father predicted of his descendants: "Dan shall judge his people, as one of the tribes of Israel. Dan shall be a serpent in the way, an adder in the path that biteth the horses' heels, so that his rider falleth backward" (**Genesis 49:17**). Dan gave birth to the territory of Canaan, including the towns of Zorah, Ajalon, Ekron, Eltekeh and ended near Joppa. His name means **"A Judge."**

Tribe #2: **ASHER**: Asher was the eighth son of Jacob. His blessings given by Jacob, his father, on his death bed, read as follows: "Out of Asher his bread shall be fat, and he shall yield royal dainties" (**Genesis 49:20**). His territory extended on the North to the northern boundary of Palestine, and on the South reached to the sough of Carmel, a length of about sixty miles. On the east it was bounded by territories of Zebulon and Naphtali, and on the west by the Mediterranean. His name means **"Happy."**

Tribe #3: **NAPHTALI**: Naphtali was the sixth son of Jacob. Jacob's wife, Rachel, gave him this name because she had wrestled in prayer for God's favor and blessings (**Genesis 30:8**). Naphtali's mother was Bilhah, Rachel's maidservant. The tribe of Naphtali settled on the north side of the tabernacle, beside those of Dan and

Asher. The territory allotted to them was in northern Palestine. It was bounded on the east by the upper Jordan and the Sea of Galilee; on the south by Issachar and Zebulun, and on the west by Zebulun and Asher. It was a long, narrow strip of land, about fifty miles from north to south, and varying from ten to fifteen miles from east to west. It is mostly mountainous and quite fertile (**Joshua 20:7**). Its boundary ran by Mount Tabor, and it numbered Ramah, Hazor, Kedesh, Iron, and Beth-anath among its fortified cities. His name means **"Obtained by Wrestling."**

Tribe #4: **MANASSEH:** Manasseh was the elder son of Joseph, and was born in Egypt. Like his brother Ephraim, he was half-Hebrew and half-Egyptian (**Genesis 41: 50 & 51**).

When Jacob desired to bless the two boys, Joseph took Ephraim in his right hand, toward Jacob's left, and Manasseh in his left, toward Jacob's right; but the dying Patriarch crossed his arms, so as to lay his right hand on Ephraim's head and his left on that of Manasseh, signifying prophetically that while both sons should become ancestors of great people, Ephraim should excel (**Genesis 48:8-12**). One half of the tribes of Manasseh joined with the tribes of Reuben and Gad in requesting permission to settle east of Jordan. The name Manasseh means **"Making to Forget."**

Tribe #5: **EPHRAIM:** Ephraim was the youngest son of Joseph. He was born while Joseph was prime minister of Egypt (**Genesis 41:45-52**). The tribe of Ephraim was allotted territory west of Jordan. Its southern boundary line ran from Jordan at Jericho to Bethel, Luz,

Ataroth-addar, upper Beth-horon, lower Beth-horon, Gezer, and the sea. The name Ephraim means **"Double Fruitfulness."**

Tribe #**6: REUBEN:** Reuben was Jacob's oldest son; the first by his wife, Leah **(Genesis 29:31 & 31).** Reuben was guilty of gross misconduct, but when his brothers plotted to kill Joseph, Reuben came forward with the proposal to cast him into a pit, designing to restore him eventually to his father. Reuben was not with his brothers when Joseph was sold to the Midianite Ishmaelite, and when visiting the pit he found it empty. Boundary of the territory of Reuben was on the east of the country of the Ammonites; on the south by the river Aron, on the west the Dead Sea and the river of Jordan. The name of Reuben means, **"Behold a Son."**

Tribe #**7: JUDAH:** Judah was the fourth son of Jacob, and also the fourth son of Leah, Jacob's wife. The tribe of Judah occupied the greater part of southern Palestine. The boundary drawn by Joshua started at the extreme southern point of the Dead Sea, then passed through by Wady-el-Fikreh, south of the ascent to Akrabbim, to the wilderness of Zin, then by the south of Kadesh-barnea and the brook of Egypt to the Mediterranean Sea. The eastern border was the Red Sea. The northern boundary started from the northern end of the sea, at the mouth of the Jordan, and passing by Beth-hoglah and near Jericho, went up by the ascent of Adummim, by En-shemesh, to Enrogl and the valley of the son of Hinnom, south of Jerusalem, passed on to Kirjath-Jearim, and then by Beth-Shemesh and Timnah, north of Ekron, to Jabneel, and on to the Mediterranean. The name of Judah means, **"Object of Praise."**

Tribe #8: **BENJAMIN:** Benjamin was the youngest of Jacob's twelve sons, and full brother of Joseph. As Jacob was approaching Bethlehem, Rachel gave birth to Benjamin, but, dying, named him Benoni, son of my sorrow. Jacob called him Benjamin (**Genesis 35:16-20)** and was deeply attached to him, especially after losing Joseph, as son of his old age and child of beloved Rachel. In the distribution of land at Shiloh, after Judah and Ephraim had received territory, the first lot came to Benjamin, who was assigned the district lying between those of Judah and Ephraim. Its northern boundary ran from Jordan through Bethel to Ataroth-addar, south of nether Beth-horon. Its western boundary ran from this point to Kiriath-Jearim. Its southern boundary went through the valley of the Dead Sea. Its eastern limit was the Jordan (**Joshua 18:11-20).** His name, **Benoni,** given by his mother on her deathbed, means, **"Son of Sorrow."** His name Benjamin, given by his father, means, **"Son of the Right Hand,"** that is, "Son of Happiness."

Tribe #9: **SIMEON:** Simeon was the second born son of Jacob by Leah (**Genesis 29:33).** In conjunction with his brother Levi, he massacred the Hivite inhabitants of Schechem on account of the injury done by one of their number to Dinah, Jacob's daughter. When one of Jacob's sons was to be kept a prisoner in Egypt as security for the return of the rest, Joseph took Simeon and bound him (**Genesis 42:24).** When the land of Canaan was distributed by lot, the second lot taken at Shiloh came forth for the tribe of Simeon, and land was assigned them in the extreme south of Canaan, in the midst of the inheritance of the children of Judah. Among the Simeonite cities were Beer-sheba, Ziklag, and Hormah in the southern part of Judah. The name Simeon means, **"Hearing."**

Tribe #10. **ISSACHAR:** Issachar was the ninth son of Jacob and the fifth by Leah **(Genesis 30:17-18).** When the land of Canaan was distributed by lot, the fourth lot taken came forth for the tribe of Issachar. Its territory was bounded on the north by Zebulun and Naphtali; on the east by Jordan; on the south and west by Manasseh and probably Asher. Jezreel and Shunem were cities that lay within its limits. The name Issachar means, **"There is Hire."**

Tribe #11: **ZEBULUN:** Zebulun was the tenth son of Jacob and the sixth by his wife, Leah **(Genesis 30:19 & 20).** He went down with his father into Egypt. After the conquest of Canaan, Zebulun was allotted territory in the northern part of the country. It lay north of Issachar; east of Asher, and south and west of Naphtali. The region possessed by Zebulun was fertile. It embraced a part of the mountainous country of Galilee and the northern and western corner of the plain of Esdraelon. Fifty thousand warriors of this tribe, with skillful and faithful commanders, went with the other tribes to Hebron to make David King (**1ᵗ Chronicles 12:33 & 40).** The name Zebulun means, **"Habitation; Dwelling."**

Tribe #12: **GAD:** Gad was a son of Jacob by Zilpah, Leah's handmaid. At his birth, Leah said, "Fortunate!" And she called his name Gad **(Genesis 30:10 & 11)**. The territory occupied by this tribe was east of Jordan, and was assigned them by Moses, but with the stipulation that, before finally settling down in it, the warriors of the tribe should cross the river with their brethren, and give assistance in the conquest of Canaan **(Numbers 32:21-32)**. The territory of the Gadites was situated between that of Reuben on the south and the half tribe of Manasseh on the north. It included the southern part of Mount Gilead from the Jabbok southward to Heshbon, and from the vicinity of Rabbath-ammon on the east westward to the Jordan valley. The name Gad means, **"Good Fortune."**

Chapter Twelve

IT IS WELL WITH MY SOUL

(At The Close of a Journey)

"If you hear someone say, H. David Parker died, tell them, 'no he did not' the last I heard him say is that 'he was going to sleep,' and when the trumpet *sounds, he was going to get up with a new body, and live eternally with the Lord." (Rev. Dr. H. David Parker)*

For the last six months, I sat quietly in my chair, not many people or family calling. I had the television on, but I paid no attention to what was playing. I did a lot of thinking. I lay down at night thinking. I looked through the obituary of my friend C.C. often; I think my wife caught me a few times, but never said anything. Every morning I said goodbye to my wife going to work and waited for her to return in the afternoon. We enjoyed a wonderful serene life, just F.D. and I. Every Tuesday I bowled with the league at Security AMF Bowling lanes; we were the lucky dozen.

The last three weeks, under the doctor's care, I discontinued bowling with the league. However, I did go and watch them for a few minutes. Once a month on Thursday, I met with my military friends at IHOP (International House of Pancakes); what a fellowship. Most days I would sit alone with my thoughts; the friends of my generation had made the ultimate transition. Hush, somebody is calling my name, was a constant sound. I still enjoyed proclaiming the Gospel of Jesus Christ; you could awake me early in the morning or late at night and I would have a sermon to preach, and I still attend service each Sunday. Some Sundays, I did not feel my best; however, I went, for the Bible states, **"forget not thyself to fellowship with the saints."** I must admit, I felt much better after making my way to the house of the Lord.

Well, on Friday, December 14, 2014, my wife, Flora, retired from her job as an adjunct professor in the Information Technology/ Computer Science Department, at the Community College of Baltimore County. It was a happy day for both of us. Now, she would be able to stay at home with me and enjoy the outings. I never asked her to retire; however, she kept cutting her hours, and then days, just to keep me company. Just before retirement, she felt the need to stay closer to me. Flora cut her hours to two a day and her days to three days a week. She was the epitome of the GOOD wife. We always enjoyed each other's company; we laughed often and shared much. Even with the age difference, we had so much in common. We would get up each morning talking and lie down at night, still talking. The two became one, "…what therefore God hath joined together, let not man put asunder." **(Matthew 19:6)** It never ceased to amaze me how much we had to share. F.D. always made me feel wonderful and young. Some days I would say, "**I cannot think and remember like I used to**." She would always say, "**Don't worry about it, you had it before**." That statement always brought a smile to my face. I would chuckle to myself and say, "Well, I guess it is okay to forget."

We started making plans for the New Year; 2015. Trips were being planned for different locations; my book would be finished. We had time now because Flora had retired from her job. We put up the Christmas tree and decorated the house; everything was beautiful. We sat back and admired our handiwork.

Now, it is coming to the close of another year. The holiday season is upon us. No one came for Christmas; we had Christmas dinner at the DoubleT Diner. With no family in Baltimore, we ate and fellowshipped with other couples for the holidays. On Friday morning, December 26th, we went to IHOP for breakfast. It was busy. The wait was not long and we sat and talked for almost an hour, about life, friends and family. We left IHOP and went to Macy's. Flora went looking for curtains. I went along with her, because lately we always stayed close to each other. Other than work, she never left my sight. She came out of Macys with absolutely nothing. We sat at home and did a few things around the house; ate dinner and relaxed by the television with a cup of green tea. As always, we watched Family Feud with Steve Harvey, Jeopardy, and Wheel of Fortune.

Well, it is time to retire for the night.

On Friday night, December 26, 2014 at around 8:15 p.m., as I was about to shower, I heard my husband struggling to breathe. I went to check on him. He took three long breaths and his head fell between his shoulders. He slipped into eternity with the Trinity. I rushed over, took his hand, called his name and then called 911. In a matter of minutes, the paramedics were here. They worked for approximately fifteen to twenty minutes, and said that they started his heart again, but I knew that his name had been called.

We went to Sinai Hospital in Baltimore. They did what they could and then put him on a respirator; normal procedures. My pastor and first lady, Reverend Emmett and Earlean Burns, met me at the hospital and they sat with me until almost 2:30 the next morning. I called my sister, Bernice, in New York; and she called his daughter, Wanda, and gave her the news. However, after enjoying Christmas in New York, his children were on their way to Baltimore to surprise Daddy, the day **after** Christmas. They got to Sinai Hospital around 3:45 a.m., Saturday morning. It was definitely a surprise, one that will never be forgotten. The Lord was with us, and in charge of everything that we did. **Life was good.** For twenty-five years, it was Mr. H. and F.D.

My sister, Bernice, and friends came on Saturday to be with me. Yes, I prayed and went to the hospital for seven days to see if the Lord had changed His mind. I do know that He does not make mistakes; just checking. On Friday, January 2, 2015, I met with the doctors, clergy, family and friends and chose to let God's divine will be done. It was the seventh day; the day of completion. We took him off the respirator, his wishes, and his life's journey on this earth ended.

Well, it is time to make major decisions: Funeral arrangements, burial, transport from Baltimore to New York, so much to do. With the Lord ordering my steps, I had two friends at Rising Sun First Baptist Church, Jean and Gwen, who took charge and made things happen. I think God for their readiness and fortitude.

A memorial service was held in Baltimore, at the Rising Sun First Baptist Church on Thursday, January 8, 2015 at 11:00 a.m. Everything went very well. However, his desire was to return to the Emanuel Baptist Church in New York for the final service and burial. This is the church where he retired as pastor after forty-five years, and was honored with the title Pastor Emeritus. It was important that his wishes were made known and fulfilled, with no shortcuts. Nothing would get in the way of saying goodbye according to the way he lived his life. I had no problem saying "no" to nonsense; it was not a time for recognition, popularity or fruitless men/women looking for publicity. All I needed around me were God-fearing pastors who had been workers in the field and knew the way of the Lord.

Strange things started happening to me, or the Lord started revealing. Nevertheless, my dreams were getting the best of me. I dreamt that on the day of the memorial in Baltimore, I could not find my way home to ride in the family car. I got lost for hours driving, trying to find a street that would lead me to one that I could recognize to get home. I was in a foreign land; everyone that I asked could not speak English and would direct me in the wrong direction. I kept driving for many more hours and never made it home. I awoke tired and exhausted, still driving....

The night after the memorial, I fell asleep again. I was in a large building with a multitude of people; a church-like setting. I was sitting on the front seat with another lady. I could see her face but did not know her name. The music started playing, "**It Is Well With My Soul.**" I found relief in singing along with the others. I was singing at the top of my voice. I had a heavy voice, no strain, just sheer delight and courageous singing. I sang most of the night and awoke still singing, "**It is well with my soul...**"

Now, I was in New York once again, on this sad occasion, waiting for the funeral at Emanuel Baptist Church. I dragged through the house, dreading the day of the service and then again waiting for it to be over. The curtain was about to close; I was yet prying, "Lord give me the strength to take **One Day At A Time**.....

We were at the wake on Monday evening, January 12th. The church, Emanuel Baptist Church of Elmont, was filled to capacity. His friend of many years, Reverend Richard Hunter, was presiding.

His faithful sons in the ministry were there, clergy friends, political leaders, community leaders, family, friends, and all those whose lives had been touched by this wonderful soldier of God. Many tributes were made befitting to his life as a living legend in ministry. The evening was long, however, everyone had an opportunity to express and remember him in his own way.

The final day was here. I could barely get myself out of bed. It was Tuesday morning, January 13th. We were on the way to the church. Three family cars: My sisters, Emma and Jeffie; two nieces and a nephew from Memphis, Reverend's sister, Ethel, her two daughters and son-in-law, the children and others. My pastor, Reverend Burns and First Lady Burns; the choir, and members from Rising Sun First Baptist Church in Baltimore attended the service. However, I entered the sanctuary with my eyes focused on the casket and my husband, whom I would see for the last time. He was lying there peaceful, sleeping; heaven was rejoicing; another saint welcomed home. Nothing could compare with this heartbreak and sudden loss. I saw people, but have no idea who was there; I heard voices but do not remember a lot of what was said. I do remember the outpouring of love from the clergy, those who were on program. Everyone was listed on the program in their respective place, just the way he contemplated it. I could almost see the smile on his face, saying, F.D., you did a great job, carrying out my wishes. I knew you could do it!

The eulogist, Reverend Herman Washington, a true friend, gave all of us everlasting hope. Lest I forget, all pastors in New York were his friends; he did so much for so many. No church was too small for him to share Jesus Christ and Him crucified. Any time he visited the Big Apple, he always had a place to preach. At the youthful age of ninety-three, he was still one of God's choice anointed. Pastors were still calling, eager to hear a word from the Lord. However, it was Reverend Herman Washington who gave him a standard date at his church, the first Sunday in February, for as long as he wanted to come.

The last time we were to go to New York, I was not able to drive, Deacon and Patricia Meadows, from Shiloh Baptist Church of Rockville Centre, were sent from New York to pick us up, and Pastor Washington brought us home himself. Many could not believe this fact when I shared it. He did it not for recognition, but because he loved God and because he admired Reverend as a friend and mentor. It was also Reverend Jesse Lyons, his Hampton Ministers' Conference, traveling friends, who invited him each year for his pastoral banquet. Friends these days are hard to fine, and certainly harder to keep.

As God's representative, for such a time as this, Reverend Herman Washington did an outstanding job, with a comparison of David and David (David, the shepherd boy, gathering the sheep in the field, and Reverend H. David, God's Shepherd, gathering the lost sheep for the cause of Christ). His subject was **"After," "Fell**

On Sleep." You had to have been there to understand the contrast; I certainly cannot repeat it correctly. At the conclusion of the message, all present can truly attest to the fact that Pastor Washington left Dr. Parker (the deceased) not dead, but asleep inside the gates of Heaven, at the foot of the Cross, waiting for the angel to come and shake him and say get up, **"Well done, thou Good and Faithful Servant....Henceforth, there is laid up for thee a crown of righteousness."** I can hear his words clearly, "I am saved because it is finished! I am sanctified, because it is finished! I am heaven bound, because it is finished! I have a crown awaiting my arrival, because it is finished." There is no doubt in my mind that he is walking around heaven; yes, perhaps, asking questions.

I am a living testimony that after the sermon, I was assured by the presence of the Holy Spirit that **everything would be all right.** As I sat there in a daze, I could hear the cherubim in loud voices singing and shouting, *Welcome! Welcome! Welcome!* I could breathe again; the load got lighter. It will take many years, but His grace is sufficient. And so now, *I rely on His grace and His mercy to watch over and protect me as I travel this road of adjustment. Yes, it is true, **"No Day Is Well Spent Without A Talk with God."***

Chapter Thirteen

EXPRESSIONS OF GRATITUDE AND PRAISE

"And I saw a new heaven and a new earth; for the first heaven and the first earth were passed away; and there was no more sea. And I, John, saw a Holy City, New Jerusalem, coming down from God out of heaven, prepared as a bride adorned for her husband. And I heard a great voice out of heaven saying, Behold the tabernacle of God is with men, and He will dwell with them, and they shall be His people, and God Himself shall be with them, and be their God." ***(Revelation 21:1-3)***

Reverend Larry W. Camp, Pastor
Bethlehem Baptist Church
Brooklyn, New York

"...a trusted and supporting friend of the Montgomery Bible Institute and Theological Center. The first chairman of the Board

*of Directors; he held this position for fifteen years. He served God faithfully the greater part of his life; almost ninety-four years. Upon his retirement from pastorate, the **B**oard honored him with the title Chairman Emeritus."*

Reverend Dr. Willie L. Muse, President
Montgomery Bible Institute and Theological Center
Montgomery, Alabama

"...a true servant for our Lord, Jesus Christ, and a great preacher. He faithfully preached the word of God and sought ever to preach the whole counsel of God. His life was a great example to the Body of Christ, his fellow clergy, and all who knew him."

Bishop Lionel Harvey, Pastor
First Baptist Cathedral of Westbury, New York

"...our family has had a relationship for many years. We praise God for blessing this servant of God with a fruitful and dedicated service to the Gospel Ministry."

Reverend Quientrell L. Burrell, Jr., Pastor
First Baptist Church
Weldon, North Carolina

"...a spiritual paradigm; his legacy of being a powerful, anointed teacher/preacher, and a man of God will remain with us forever. He

made an impact in the lives of individuals within the Church, the community and the Metropolitan area."

Reverend Joe L. Brown, Pastor
Faith Baptist Church
Hempstead, New York

"...a reverent man of prayer who loved the Lord. A very loyal and faithful person who served his family, and set a good example. He loved his family with a gentle, yet stern combination which only he possessed. He was a confident counselor and closest of friends. He was a person who was always available to share an encouraging word and demonstrate strong support to those in need."

Bishop Shelton C. Daniel, Pastor and Founder
Greater Joy Baptist Church
Rocky Mount, North Carolina

"...whereas, the golden bells have tolled for our brother-in-Christ, Union is proud to count among its sons in the gospel ministry the Reverend H. David Parker who began his ordained Christian journey at the Union Baptist Church of Hempstead where he came an ordained deacon. We thank the Lord for his life, his service, and his influence. A 'life's race well run; a life's work well done; a life's crown well won.'"

Reverend Dr. Sedgwick V. Easley, Pastor
Union Baptist Church
Hempstead, New York

"...his life was a life of the highest and noblest ideals, and the light of his Christian character was shed upon all with whom he came in contact. We feel that the uplifted Christian influence of his life will live forever. Though he has transition, he has left a living example of loving service worthy of our emulation."

Reverend Dr. Norman Wallace Scott, Pastor

Rising Star Baptist Church

Jamaica, New York

"...a faithful and dedicated servant of the Lord. A true Christian, who enjoyed sharing his wisdom and knowledge of God's Word. He will be fondly remembered and missed for his easy smile, sense of humor, cooperative spirit and humble demeanor. His strength, faith, devotion to family, church and community, and his determination to serve the Lord will remain steadfast in our memories. "Precious in the sight of the LORD is the death of his saints." (Psalm 116:15)

Reverend Dr. Emmett C. Burns, Pastor and Founder

Rising Sun First Baptist Church

Baltimore, Maryland

"...a great pulpiteer, pastor and preacher. He will truly be missed throughout the Christian Community. The Apostle Peter encourages us to "Cast our cares upon Him for He carest for us." (I Peter 5:7)

Rev. Gilbert Pickett, Sr., Pastor & Overseer

Mount Horeb Baptist Church

Corona, New York

"...his pastor emeritus, who nobly served the church, and larger community entrusted to his spiritual care with a depth of love and commitment moved from labor to reward. We honor and celebrate his compassion, his uncommonly brotherly love and support.

Reverend Jeffery S. Thompson, Pastor

Amity Baptist Church

Jamaica, New York

"...the very fine and distinguished pastor of the Emanuel Baptist Church of Elmont for some forty-five years. A pillar in the Elmont, Hempstead and surrounding communities. He inspired many to achieve higher and nobler things in life."

Reverend Phillip McDowell, Pastor

South Hempstead Baptist Church

Hempstead, New York

"...it is with great joy and rejoicing that God has allowed an awesome gospel preacher, a father figure, a family friend, a confidant, to pass this way and touch our lives. He has been an intricate part of my ministry and family life in so many positive ways."

Reverend Richard Hunter, Pastor

First African Baptist Church

Eufaula, Alabama

"...a man of dignity and godly character; a man of wisdom and knowledge a well as saturated in the Baptist doctrine. A man with an excellent spirit; one who shared the Gospel messages throughout the tristate area, and also on the national level. He was a renowned Christian educator and theologian. We thank for having known him for at least fifty years as my pastor and father in the ministry."

Reverend Ronald Simpkins, Pastor
Freewheel Baptist Church
Jamaica, New York

"...a giant among men; the voice of one crying in the wilderness; a dear friend and confidant; one loved and admired by so many; a shining example of a Christian man, and a spiritual mentor. He has left a great void in the Christian community, and we at Shiloh have been sorely impacted by this loss. It was always good to be in his presence."

Reverend Herman Washington, Pastor
Shiloh Baptist Church
Rockville Centre, New York

"...a faithful and dedicated servant of the Lord; serving the Emanuel Baptist Church, community, county, state and nationally. We pause to give tribute to the memory and legacy of this devoted man of God. His years of immeasurable and selfless service will live on in the hearts and minds of those with whom he came in contact."

Reverend Ralph P. Taylor, Pastor
Emanuel Baptist Church
Elmont, New York

"...I have no doubt that a man of his caliber, who dedicated his life to the work of the Lord and mentored so many ministers, myself included, is resting with the Lord. I rejoice that I was blessed to have known, to have loved, and been mentor to by such an awesome man of God."

Reverend Henry Faison, Jr., Pastor
First Baptist Church of Southampton
Southampton, New York

"...The body of Christ has suffered a tremendous loss of a faithful and devoted servant, whose life emulated the glory of God."

Reverend Preston H. Drinks, Pastor
Second Baptist Church
Baldwin, New York

"...a great man of God; a wonderful and loving pastor and friend; a dynamic preacher and teacher of the Gospel of Jesus Christ. A true servant of Jesus Christ, who devoted his time and served faithfully all the days of his life. He unselfishly gave of himself, his time, and resources to encourage, nurture, develop, and provide for all that he came in contact."

Reverend Dr. Eric Charles Mallette, Pastor
Greater Second Baptist Church
Freeport, New York 11520

"..he was like Enoch who walked with God. His life was one of biblical truth, and conviction. He lived a life of non-conformity; those

of us who knew him will remember him as a vessel God used consistently and effectively for many years."

Reverend Edward Corley, Pastor
Mount Olive Baptist Church
Manhasset, New York

"...a faithful member of the Antioch Baptist Church of Hempstead; it was at Antioch that he demonstrated a sincere and obedient walk with God. A son of the Antioch Baptist Church the Cathedral of God; having served as the first assistant pastor. Our beloved was a community leader who loved and supported his family, friends and neighbors.

Bishop Phillip E. Elliott, Pastor
Antioch Baptist Church of Hempstead
Hempstead, New York

"There was a man sent from God, whose name was John. The same came for a witness, to bear witness of the Light that all men through him might believe. He was not that Light, but was sent to bear witness of that Light."

Reverend Kent M. Edmonston, Pastor
Mt. Olive Baptist Church
Oyster Bay, New York

"I had never met a man of God like the Reverend H. David Parker. He was loving, firm and he was serious. Reverend Parker was a major force in my spiritual life and walk with the Lord. I remember riding in the car with Dr. Parker and having a one on one conversation with him about ministry. Dr. Parker said, "Brother Butler, I believe that I am a pretty good pastor; I believe that I can get people to follow; I am a pretty good administrator and every once in a while, I give a good sermon." It was not all about him; it was about the Lord and people having a personal relationship with him. In 1995, Dr. Parker gave me the opportunity to preach my trial sermon. He did not present me with my license at that time, because he wanted to make sure that my head would not get too big. I loved working with and learning from this man of God. My life has not been the same since the passing of my pastor; he was a great inspiration to me. I thank God for allowing me the great privilege to serve under him for eleven years as an associate minister and having him as a part of my life for twenty-two years.

Reverend Dr. Donald E. Butler, Pastor
Community Baptist Church,
Southampton, L.I., New York

THE AUTHOR

Reverend Herbert David Parker was a husband, father, teacher, builder and leader par excellence, who faithfully and successfully led the Emanuel Baptist Church congregation for forty-five years. He was a messenger for Christ for fifty-one years, and a friend to mankind. Because of his love and devotion for Christ, our lives are the richer.

H. David Parker was a living testimony that a man of God can be strong and yet still maintain humility. He firmly stated, "This is God's Church, not mine. I cannot get you into Heaven, but I can tell you how to get there." He was a humble servant; modest, not boastful, who often let the people know that he was just an instrument, used by God, pointing souls to Christ.

He was not ashamed of the Gospel. He stood committed and dedicated to the word of God. His favorite Scripture was, "For I am not ashamed of the Gospel of Christ: for it is the power of God unto salvation to everyone that believeth; to the Jew first, and also to the Greek." (**Romans 1:16**)

Because of God's grace and mercy, Dr. Parker's life was one of dedication and commitment. On Sunday, you could find him preaching the Gospel of Jesus Christ. Monday through Friday, you could find him counseling and telling others about the goodness of God, and sharing his life experiences. And on Saturday, you could find him teaching the inspired Word of God.

He was courageous in action and fervent in prayer. He did not alter God's Word. In this modern-day society, he would let us know that the wages of sin is still death, but the gift of God is eternal life through Christ Jesus.

As a pastor, he was the epitome of leadership, being steadfast, unmovable, always abounding in the Word of the Lord. He abounded in love, and proclaimed the Gospel message wherever he went that God would receive the glory. Throughout his writings, you will read about his accomplishments and leadership abilities in community service, nationally and internationally.

Reverend H. David Parker was a giant who walked among giants, yet he still took time to compliment and encourage the little children, as he often did when he acknowledged their accomplishments during morning service. He was a man of character, integrity, dignity and honesty. He took literally the motto of Emanuel: "In Emanuel Everybody is Somebody, and Christ is All." He was a visionary; a man after God's own heart. It was his vision that brought into being a $3 million edifice, the New Emanuel Baptist Church. It was paid for through his vision and leadership. With

much prayer, he insisted that payments be made God's way, with tithes and offerings. God honored his faithfulness.

Reverend Herbert David Parker was a man of wisdom. He has now made the eternal transition, from Earth to Heaven. His niece, E. Faye Wright, gave these expressions: *"If we asked most people how they would describe their loved ones, they will say, they are best in the world. Well, I concur when speaking of my Uncle He was an amazing man. His greatest quality, to me, was sonable he was. He was a very quiet person, yet his ver spoke volumes; this was his gift, young or old; ever be near him. He was at his best when he preached His excitement, when bringing the Word, was throughout the room. It always left you want every time! He was a very humble man, so likable, a very calm demeanor.*

"If we only knew that the last tim the last time we would see them hug them a little bit tighter.

"The funniest memory v sweets, for it did not matt gum. He would alway sweet. I am blessed

Reverend H. self; to be better carried out his pastoral

CPSIA information can be obtained
at www.ICGtesting.com
Printed in the USA
BVOW11s2056130616

451903BV00003B/3/P